DERBYSHIRE'S HIGH PEAK

AIR CRASH SITES

NORTHERN REGION

Books by the Author

Non-fiction
Bomb on the Red Markers
Fighter! Fighter! Corkscrew Port!
The Fear In the Sky
Through Enemy Skies
We Kept 'Em Flying

Peakland Air Crash Series:
The South (2005)
The Central Area (2006)
The North (2006)

Derbyshire's High Peak Air Crash Sites, Northern Region
High Peak Air Crash Sites, Central Region
Derbyshire's High Peak Air Crash Sites, Southern Region
White Peak Air Crash Sites

Faction
A Magnificent Diversion Series
(Acclaimed by the First World War Aviation Historical Society)
The Infinite Reaches 1915–16
Contact Patrol 1916
Sold A Pup 1917
The Great Disservice 1918

Blind Faith: Joan Waste, Derby's Martyr
Joyce Lewis of Mancetter, Lichfield's Feisty Martyr

Fiction
In Kinder's Mists (a Kinderscout ghost story)
Though the Treason Pleases (Irish Troubles)

DERBYSHIRE'S HIGH PEAK
AIR CRASH SITES
NORTHERN REGION

Pat Cunningham, DFM

'I give you a GPS for Christmas and you turn into a bloody anorak'

Wiesława White

Front-cover image: Walkers, Ian Pell and Melvyn Stephenson, Holme Moss

First published 2014 by DB Publishing, an imprint of JMD Media Ltd, Nottingham, United Kingdom.

ISBN 9781780913735

Printed and bound by Copytech (UK) Limited, Peterborough.

Contents

Private publications by the Author

'Now We Are Ninety' (tribute to mother ...)

'The Elephant Box, Volumes 1 # 2' (a grandfather's tall tales)

'By Fell and Dale, Volumes 1 # 5' (walker's logs)

'Frozen Tears' (a Polish family's wartime odyssey)

'Flotsam' (short pieces)

'Jetsam' (short pieces)

Autobiographical Series:

'Brat to Well Beloved' (RAF Aircraft Apprentice to Air Electronics Officer)

[And, vice Gilbert and Sullivan ...]

'Apprentice to a Pilot' (RAF pilot training)

'The Kind Commander' (RAF captaincy)

'The Simple Captain' (civil captaincy)

In preparation:

'Frozen Tears' (wartime romance)

'The Ignorant Walker's Companion' (a walker's reflections)

'The Tenant'/'The CEO' (experiences of a housing association)

'Fifty Years Of Peace: 1945-1995' [Celebratory Stones in Derbyshire] (Memoirs of RAF 'peacekeeping' personnel from Malaya to the First Gulf War)

***Pat Cunningham,
DFM, BA, Lic Ac, cfs, RAF, 2014***

INTRODUCTION

The upland moors which feature in this book show regional variations which are in marked contrast to the overall similarity of the terrain found on the Bleaklow and Kinder moorlands to the south where, seen from afar, the appearance of dark, peaty tops speaks for itself. Here, in the north, the dramatically scenic, straw-hued hills of the Castleshaw, Saddleworth, and Wessenden Head Moors, though predominantly heather moorlands, prove also to be the spawning ground of monstrous stretches of tufted grass that can make off-path walking a Herculean labour. These, however give way in the west to the rock-strewn, heathered vasts of Tintwistle, to the dark and deeply fissured peat around Dovestone Reservoir, and to the far more kindly cotton-grasses of the Sliddens, Tooleyshaw, and Westend Mosses south of Black Hill. Off to the east, on the other hand, where in ancient times Northern Mercia – the geographical focus of Peakland – extended beyond the high ground, the land is essentially pastoral.

In all zones, however, walking trails abound, as exemplified by the two which leave Crowden for Black Hill, the Pennine Way lifting to one of the finest of rock-edge walks, and the less-well-defined and largely grassy track curving eastwards to take an equally airy route over White Moss. Even so, the walker will find reminders enough that Moss translates as bog! Just the same, with such a variety of good paths, visiting one of the many air-crash sites rarely requires more than a twenty-minute excursion from a regular track.

As for the sheer number of crash sites, virtually all were caused because cloud-shrouded crews had set out from sea-level aerodromes and were unaware that they had drifted off track over high moorland. They were, therefore, erroneously confident that the 2,000-foot reading on their altimeters meant they had that much clear air beneath them.

The upland walker, then, should set aside all thoughts of mystery in relation to the sites. Certainly, to the aviator-walker, the true interest in them lies in the flight-safety lessons they taught those who followed on. No mystery disasters, then; not a single cover-up; no falsified official reports; and not a conspiracy theory in sight. Not even a ghost.

Some moorland sites can be accessed from road level, notably at Holme Moss, at 1,700 feet above sea level. But even to reach the Chew Valley heights, raised 1,500 feet above the Dovestone Reservoir, demands little more than an hour's climb. Then again, such ascents invariably lead up picturesque valleys, at the head of which the walker is freed from further true labour – until the ultimate, knee-straining descent! –, the upland paths gently undulating to offer wide and ever-changing prospects.

Off path, of course, the heather, bracken, tussock grass, and blanket bogs common to all these moorlands can make tortuous going. And, as always, water continually moulds the landscape, cutting through peat to the bed-rock in water channels known as groughs which leave above them the heathery islets known as hags. As always too, although in many areas singular rock features stud the landscape – to say nothing of the Holme Moss television mast soaring above all as a fair-visibility locator –, there are stretches where the off-path walker gets the impression of traversing a vast and featureless wilderness.

In truth, however, none of these moors is really that extensive, few being more than a thirty-minute trek from an unmistakable major path or road. However, whether higher or lower in elevation, they can jealously demand respect. Sensible clothing is a must. Then again, fogs can fall with startling rapidity, when a proven facility with map and compass can ease the mind no end. In such conditions a little time spent getting the 'inbuilt sense of direction' under control can pay dividends; 'Trust your instruments', as fliers learn from the cradle. If invariably acknowledging the caveat, 'Unless they've gone wrong.' And, of course, a GPS, ideally with mapping, and a breadcrumb trail to show where you've safely been, can be a godsend.

Even in good weather, however, care should be exercised. The summit of Black Hill provides a good example, its inverted-basin slopes hiding all the downwards routes, so that only a compass bearing and map will ensure that, for example, the Crowden Path is taken, and not that leading off towards Dean Head Moss: the map says nothing about which is paved … Add mist to the equation and the problem becomes infinitely magnified.

Studying the proposed route beforehand, not least on Google Earth, is time well spent. As is giving notice of your intended route. And anticipating mobile-phone coverage to be poor.

Many walkers will require only the guaranteed coordinates given, just the same, a walkers' guide follows each narrative, and in two cases where the sites are just off the popular Dark Peak sheet, a sketch map. The associated GPS-derived elevation, however, is best regarded as merely a rough indicator. The same for any timings given.

Spurious air-crash sites

In the main, these derive from local lore which, in turn, has been embodied in the various lists compiled by zeal-led air-crash enthusiasts. Some, however, have seemingly impeccable provenances, and have been actively searched for over many years. Certainly, in the interests of creating a definitive record of air crashes in the area, each supposed crash had to be investigated by interviews combined with archive delving and site visits. A few were deemed worthy of future research, but discounting those found spurious will save other site-seekers both time and frustration, allowing them to concentrate instead on the myriad natural delights the northern moorlands have to offer.

The air-crash debris

What the walker will see at most sites is a tiny pool of debris, often set in very broken terrain. For this reason, although the coordinates supplied are accurate, it may well be necessary to search about in order to locate the debris pool.

Of course, a pile of aluminium added to or subtracted from by generations of walkers does not necessarily indicate the actual impact site. For when an aircraft bellied into the moor at cruising speed, the debris was often sprayed over hundreds of yards; far further after an explosion.

In other cases, when aircraft have struck rock faces, what debris remains tends to be pooled on lower ground. Then again, to avoid distracting later air searches, the salvage parties tumbled what they could not destroy into the nearest gully and buried it. Yet air-crash enthusiasts squabble over an inch or two!

There is also much enthusiast wrangling about what they choose to regard as the sanctity of the sites. Yet there was never any intention of the debris becoming enshrined. What aircraft parts are to be seen now have largely been disinterred by earlier enthusiasts. Then again it has to be evident to all that on more accessible ground – as in the east of this northern region – air-crash sites were returned to the plough the moment the salvage teams departed, and only in rare cases was even an unofficial memorial raised. This walker-aviator, for his part, would like to see the Ministry of Defence (the inheritors of the sites) clear the moors of all such debris, conceivably, leaving a tasteful memorial marker to record the individual tragedy.

A further reflection, flying blindly into – or more frequently, being flown into – high ground does not, of itself, confer upon those haplessly involved either courage or heroism. In fact, a hoary aircrew aphorism covers the case admirably, though best transposed here as, 'Just their 'orrible luck.'

Pseudo-sentiment aside, it is accepted that some walkers are only interested in air-crash sites where there is debris – or a memorial – to give focus to a high-moorland walk. Yet to the walker with a deeper aviation interest, sites with no surface debris often have more to offer than those still littered with shards of metal.

Certainly, all crash sites in the series, whether fully or more slightly covered, have been equally proven by metal-detector findings, by contemporary photographs, and by verifiable witness reports.

Regarding technicalities in the text, it is hoped that those not made self-evident will be covered in the glossary, but the intrusive 'see Glossary' is only rarely employed.

Pat Cunningham, DFM, 2014 (RAF 1951 – 1973)

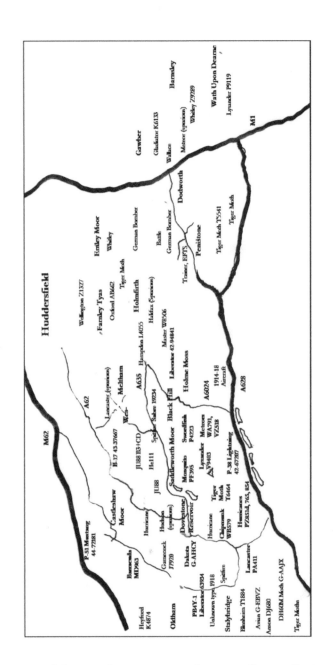

Map of the Northern Region showing the crash sites

These are crash sites where debris remained on the surface in 2013; in one case where a memorial has been erected.

Castleshaw Moor Area

1. North American P-51D Mustang 44-72181
Castleshaw Moor, north-east of Oldham

SD 99902 11184 403 m

Unit and Station: United States Eighth Army Air Force, 2nd Air Division, 4th Fighter Group, 336th Fighter Squadron, Army Air Force (AAF) 356 (RAF Debden), near Saffron Walden, south of Cambridge.

Date: 29 May 1945

Crew: pilot, killed – First Lieutenant Harold H. Frederick, United States Army Air Force

North American P-51 Mustang

Mustang foursome

On 8 May 1945 the Second World War in Europe ended, but with the Japanese War still raging it was decided to redeploy a number of Mustang long-range escorts to the Far East. The first stage in this transfer was to position the aircraft to Speke, the airfield most convenient for the Liverpool docks. On 29 May 1945, therefore, a fleet of twenty-three Mustangs took

off from RAF Debden – AAF 356 – on the 160 mile ferry. What followed turned into a debacle, but complicated as the situation became, the seeds of that debacle had been sown before departure, permitting hindsight to be legitimately used to identify some of the errors made, and to follow the vagaries of fortune that attended the ill-starred operation.

First Lieutenant Harold H. Frederick

The Senior Operations Officer of 4th Fighter Group had personally assigned command of the formation to a First Lieutenant Harold H. Frederick, a relatively experienced pilot with just under a thousand hours of flying, of which some four hundred were combat time. First Lieutenant Frederick had been shot down over Évreux in June 1944 but had been returned by the French Resistance via Spain, had since led the 4th Fighter Group on a wartime mission, and was presently holding the post of Assistant Operations [Intelligence] Officer for the 336th Fighter Squadron. Group Operations staff, therefore, having ensured that he was provided with a fair proportion of experienced pilots for the lift, left him to make his own arrangements.

First Lieutenant Frederick decided to operate the aircraft from all the three squadrons involved as a single formation. This was no great matter in itself, for by splitting the twenty-three aircraft into elements of five double-pairs and a single threesome, each element leader would be ultimately responsible for his own section. In truth, organising the lift was not a particularly onerous task; given good weather and a reasonable degree of luck.

However, there was to be no good weather, for on the morning of the flight, cloud was heaped upon the high ground on route, while showers, scud, and industrial haze reduced the visibility at Liverpool. Just the same, Group Operations approved the choice of a direct routing over the Peak District. For his part, First Lieutenant Frederick gave a comprehensive pre-take-off brief, even detailing the parking of the aircraft at Speke. Several pilots, however, later recorded that he described the terrain on the direct route (across the Peak District!) as 'flat and level'.

As take-off time approached the Group Operations Officer – ultimately responsible for the whole operation – was advised that the poor-visibility conditions had barely altered in the Liverpool area. But although he would later criticise his appointed leader for not checking the latest met before departing – and for not administratively clearing the flight in quite the approved manner! – the senior officer seems to have made no move to get this daunting information passed on to First Lieutenant Frederick, still less to delay the formation, which duly got airborne at 1005 hours.

As would have been expected of a flight into frontal conditions, it proved necessary to climb steadily in order to remain in clear skies, so that on passing Leicester the formation was at 6,000 feet over unbroken cloud. What could not have been anticipated was that a microphone should jam on, effectively blocking the communications channel for the whole formation. And this persisted throughout the flight, for when a frequency change was effected the inadvertently offending aircraft merely changed too. Strangely, however, although the flight was to cruise north-westwards for some forty-five minutes more, no action was taken to identify, and so eliminate, the inhibiting interference.

But all went well until, using time-and-distance reckoning alone, First Lieutenant Frederick closed the formation up, and began to lead them down by sections through the now unbroken overcast. What followed has to chill the blood of any modern flier, but the reported experience of just two elements, Red and Blue Sections, will paint the picture.

An element of two pairs flying in left-hand finger-four formation

The leader of Red Section descended his element to 2,400 feet on his altimeter, then, still in thick cloud, levelled off, looking for a hole. Not seeing one, he eased down further, and eventually broke cloud in rain and industrial smoke at an estimated 1,000 ft above Burtonwood airfield. Despite the jammed microphone (and most likely aided by sheer proximity) he managed to contact Burtonwood and get a heading for Speke, where he landed. His number four, having advised amid all this that he was flying wide to the left of the element in the descent because of a control-trim problem, heard the heading passed for Speke, adopted it, followed it through the gloom, and actually managed to rejoin Red Section before the landing; making Red Section's a very creditable, if decidedly nail-biting, effort all round!

Blue Section, the next in line to descend, was not so fortunate. Blue Leader led his element down to 1,500 feet on his altimeter, but finding himself still in cloud powered up and began to climb out again. In so doing, however, he lost his three followers, and did not break clear himself until 9,000 feet. Once on top, and now alone, he found a gap, and recognising Manchester, made a visual descent. But even having crept beneath the cloud he failed in three attempts to reach Speke and once again climbed, this time being forced up to 11,000 feet before rediscovering clear air. Finally, getting a heading for Speke from Burtonwood, and once more descending as best he could, he managed to locate the field, and landed; to receive the news that his number four, Flight Officer Darnaby Wilhoit, had fatally crashed (See page 140, *High Peak Air Crash Sites, Central Region*).

First Lieutenant Frederick's element. In the descent numbers three and four separated as a pair, but on encountering cloud-covered high ground split up themselves. Number three subsequently rejoined the by-then damaged number two and returned in company with him to Debden, where number four also landed

This narrative, however, follows the fortunes of the overall formation leader, First Lieutenant Frederick, and the threesome he had led down through cloud. Failing to locate Speke he had duly climbed again, but on breaking clear at about 10,000 feet discovered that he had lost his numbers three and four. Just the same, he set himself up to make a further attempt with his number two, First Lieutenant Beacham Brooker, unaware as he did so that in the course of repositioning he had drifted north-eastwards, and that as he descended once more he was, in fact, a full forty miles away from sea-level Speke, and over the 1,300-feet-above-sea-level moorlands beyond Oldham.

So it transpired that his number two, still grittily sticking to his leader's starboard wing, with mist streaking past in his peripheral vision, suddenly saw the other's aircraft disintegrate in a 'ball of fire', felt a jar on his own port wing, and pulled aside, not climbing for height, but holding low, preferring to keep even doubtful visual contact with the ground rather than risk an instrument climb in his damaged state.

First Lieutenant Beacham Brooker's damaged wingtip

First Lieutenant Beacham Brooker

Settling, the erstwhile number two could see that his left wingtip was badly crumpled. A slow-speed handling check, however, proved that he had control enough to land safely, and when he then fell into company with his number three, by now himself a singleton, both of them turned for Debden, where their number four had already made a safe arrival. They were to find that the rest of the formation, bar First Lieutenant Frederick and Flight Officer Wilhoit, had either probed their various hazardous ways, in pairs or as singletons, into Speke or, like them, had aborted the mission and returned to Debden.

Tragically, First Lieutenant Harold Frederick's aircraft had indeed exploded in flames as it struck Castleshaw Moor, further disintegrating as it bellied over the hummocks, giving him no chance of surviving whatsoever.

But neither was he to be given any better chances back at base. For the Senior Group Operations Officer, in an ostensibly chest-baring statement, appeared to take full blame upon himself, reporting that 'The entire mission was poorly managed by the Group Operations Officer who accepted too many factors without closer scrutiny'. He then contritely observed that the mission should 'not have been left to independent units', and that a less than thorough supervision had been exercised. He further wrote of the rigorous control of flying activities he intended to exercise in the future, stoutly confessing, 'This does not excuse the previous laxity that is considered to be a major factor contributing to the disastrous accidents.'

And then, in the interests of showing just how remiss he had been in ever appointing First Lieutenant Frederick to the lead, he charged that the lieutenant, in addition to not having correctly booked out, and not having updated his met information, had, through his lack of judgement in not aborting the mission in view of the weather and the lack of radio contact, been one hundred percent responsible for the accident; indeed for all the accidents and incidents alike.

This apparently career-sacrificing *mea culpa*, however, fell just a little short of convincing when his immediate superior reported upwards, pointing out that the worthy Senior Group Operations Officer 'had just taken over the operational duty and was not responsible on the day of this incident and ... that the previous operations officer had failed to take proper supervisory action': that he, as commanding general, had neither taken, nor even contemplated taking, any disciplinary action against his new Senior Group Operations Officer.

On the other hand First Lieutenant Frederick's squadron commander, whose involvement in the matter seems minimal, to say the least, was immediately relieved of his post and sent packing to the United States. The commanding general did, however, amend the new Senior Group Operations Officer's percentage of cause, apportioning it as 30% to supervisory personnel, 20% to the weather, and only 50% attributable to the flight leader.

At the crash site there may be some additional interest to the aircraft-enthusiast walker in that the particular P-51D in which First Lieutenant Frederick flew to his death had, until that ferry, been the personal aircraft of Colonel Everitt W. Stewart, the 4th Fighter Group's revered commander from February until September 1945. Dubbed '*Sunny VIII*', it had been resplendently maintained, but although some elements of it still remained at the crash site in 2013, no paintwork, not even its eleven swastika victory-symbols, had survived, only crumpled aluminium sheets and riveted spars, often enough hidden from sight by the rough and seasonally haylike hummock-grasses of wind-razed Castleshaw Moor.

Mustang 44-72181, Castleshaw Moor, 2013, showing hummock grass

VISITING THE SITE

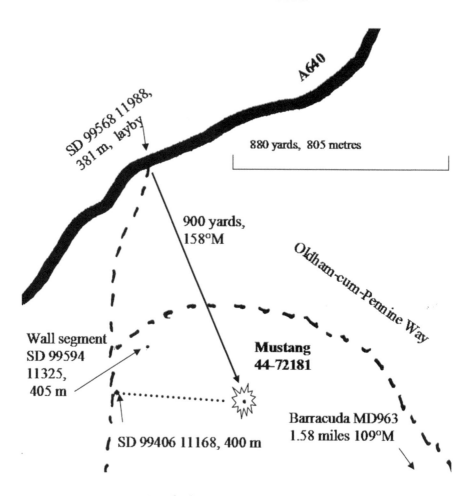

Castleshaw Mustang site map

Convenient parking is provided by a two-car lay-by on the A640 (Huddersfield-Denshaw Road) at SD 99568 11988, 381 metres, diagonally across the way from a museum-piece cast-iron signpost giving the immediate location as the 'Huddersfield & Newhey Road, Friarmere'. The map, and a public-footpath sign to Castleshaw Moor, show a footpath leading off towards the nearby Oldham Way. And from the level of the lay-by a trail on the ground may indeed be discerned leading off on 215°M. Certainly, the formulated plan might be to follow this indicated footpath to and past its intersection with the Oldham Way before, at SD 99406 11168, heading east to the crash-site coordinates given (SD 99902 11184 403 m).

Unfortunately, although the Oldham Way is distinctive enough on the ground, with a drystone-wall corner piece at SD 99594 11325, 405 metres, to provide a singular aiming point on the skyline, the connecting footpath, at best, seems to be a mapmaker's conceit. Further, as with so many of these northern moors, malevolently-minded tussock grass abounds. Because of which, rather than seeking to find an illusory footpath, it might be as well to set a course direct for the site from the lay-by (say 158°M) and soldier it out during the 900-yard, thirty-minute, off-path trek this takes.

Then again, once at the location, the ground is so broken and the grasses, at any season, so lush, that it may well be necessary to cast around in order to spot the debris. On the plus side, the scenery well repays the effort, although this is best viewed when taking a breather, the ankle-turning tussocks which give the straw-shaded slopes their deceptively inviting appearance demanding care at every step.

Some walkers on a round-trip outing might combine this crash-site visit with one to that of Barracuda MD963 (see below), which lies 1.58 miles distant on a heading of 109°M, although a section of the Pennine-cum-Oldham Way might be utilised.

2. Fairey Barracuda Mk.3 MD963
Redbrook Clough, Close Moss, Marsden

SE 02365 10445 367 m

Unit and Station: Royal Navy, Station Flight,
Royal Naval Air Station Dunino, south-east of St Andrews

Date: 29 July 1945

Crew: solo pilot, killed:

- Sub-Lieutenant George Henry Ambler, Royal Naval Air Service

Fairey Barracuda

The Barracuda was designed as a three-seater torpedo-bomber and reconnaissance aircraft for the Royal Navy. Although unprepossessing in appearance, and with its design performance degraded by the heavy components called for by the Admiralty's specification for carrier operations, the Barracuda was still a step up from the Swordfish and Albacore types it replaced. But while the Barracuda gave yeoman service there is the adage, as old as aviation itself, which holds that if an aeroplane looks good, it flies good. Only surely even the Barracuda's own designer cannot have thought much of its looks! Although judging by the number of female ferry pilots photographed while operating the type there may be some element here of the beast attracting the beauty.

Air Transport Auxiliary (ATA) pilot Maureen Dunlop having delivered a Barracuda

An ATA pilot carries out a pre-flight inspection on a Barracuda

When it was destroyed on 29 July 1945, Fairey Barracuda MD963 was on the strength of Royal Naval Air Station Dunino, south-east of St Andrews, Fife. Further, its pilot, Sub-Lieutenant George Ambler, was on a solo detail. Beyond this, though, nothing more was established regarding the prelude to this fatality.

A Mr J.W. Wood, of nearby Bleak Hey Nook, however, witnessed the final moments of the Barracuda's flight. He was walking on Close Moss when a very low-flying aeroplane suddenly appeared out of the overcast. His impression was that the pilot saw the ground and immediately began a tight, avoiding turn. As the aircraft banked, however, Mr Walker was horrified to see it falter, then plummet into the ground, and explode in flames.

It is evident that Sub-Lieutenant Ambler, suddenly aware of his peril, pulled hard, away from the ground; but pulled too harshly, and straight into the judder of a high-speed stall, totally defeating his object – that of turning rapidly – as the turn rate faltered and a wing dropped. Restoration of the turn required the merest relaxation on the stick, only with a hillside looming that luxury was denied the hapless Sub-Lieutenant Ambler.

In 2013 the crash site retained a surprising amount of wreckage considering its proximity to a footpath.

The debris of Barracuda MD963 in 2013, with Redbrook Clough and the Carriage House pub

VISITING THE SITE

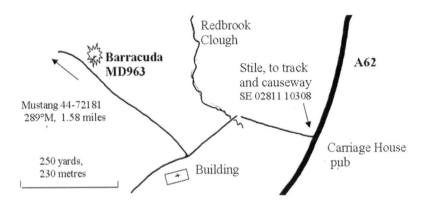

Map of the Barracuda site

Having sought permission, convenient parking is to be found at the Carriage House Public House on the A62 to the south-west of Marsden. The crash site will then take some fifteen minutes to reach. A convenient stile at SE 02811 10308, immediately across the road from the pub, gives the walker access to a causeway which crosses Redbrook Clough and leads to a large industrial blockhouse building. On reaching this structure a well-defined path leads off on 299°M for 290 yards, undulating slightly until the site is seen just feet to the right of the path. There is a moderate amount of debris bounded by a stone circle.

The alternative, parking on the nearest lay-by down the A62 (Marsden to Oldham Road), necessitates either an unpleasant juggernaut-braving roadside trek, or an even more unpleasant trackless negotiation of the steep-sided clough and its boggy hummock grass. Other walkers, however, may well take in this site together with that of Mustang 44-72181 (see below) on Castleshaw Moor, just over a mile and a half to the north-west (basically 289°M), possibly utilising, in part, a segment of the Pennine-cum-Oldham Way.

3. Boeing B-17G 43-37667
Meltham Moor (south-west of Huddersfield)

SE 07088 09526 426 m

Unit and Station: United States Eighth Army Air Force,
447th Bombardment Group, 709th Bombardment Squadron,
AAF126 (RAF Rattlesden), Stowmarket, Suffolk
Date: 6 April 1945
Crew: five, United States Army Air Force, all injured, two seriously:

- First Lieutenant Winston Johnson, pilot, fractured spine
- Second Lieutenant Raymond W. Parks, co-pilot
- Second Lieutenant Walter Vukelic, navigator, fractured spine
- Sergeant Robert J. Schnug, flight engineer
- Sergeant Robert J. Woodbeck, radio operator

Boeing B-17 Flying Fortress

All aircraft require periodic servicing, and on occasion relatively major modification as components are changed at the end of their useful life. So it was that on 6 April 1945 it became necessary to run in – the American term was to 'slow time' – two newly-fitted engines on B-17G 43-37667. This merely involved flying off a certain number of hours, so on volunteering for the task First Lieutenant Winston Johnson stood down his four gunners and Second Lieutenant Dick Kinder, his bombardier, as surplus to the flight. For the rest of the crew the duty probably offered a relaxing break after the six missions (the RAF term was 'operations') they had flown over Germany since arriving in the United Kingdom a month before.

The truncated crew. Left to right, standing: Sergeant Robert J. Schnug, flight engineer; Sergeant Robert J. Woodbeck, radio operator. Kneeling: First Lieutenant Winston Johnson, pilot; Second Lieutenant Raymond W. Parks, co-pilot; Second Lieutenant Walter Vukelic, navigator

The truncated crew duly got airborne at 1730 hours, and after a while, to escape the monotony of simply cruising around the local area, decided to head off to Manchester. As they approached the Southern Pennines, however, the weather deteriorated, and with the visibility decreasing and the under-surface of the cloud forcing them ever lower in order to maintain visual contact with the ground, they realised that they were lost. First Lieutenant Johnson, with the aircraft flying in a rain-fringed cloud base that varied from just 400 to 600 feet above ground level, handed control to his co-pilot, Second Lieutenant Parks, and joined the navigator in the nose in what proved to be a vain endeavour to obtain a visual fix.

First Lieutenant Johnson had just decided to resort to their Gee radar-lattice navigational aid, and so positively determine their position, when the co-pilot, suddenly seeing hills looming to one side, powered up into a climb. The machine at once entered cloud but before the co-pilot could fully settle onto instruments it flew into the moorland sloping upwards from below.

On impact the climbing B-17 slowed rapidly, shedding components in a lengthy uphill slide until a wingtip dug in and slewed it violently, bringing it to an abrupt halt, with fire breaking out just moments later. The co-pilot, the engineer, and the radio operator, all only slightly injured, evacuated hurriedly; to discover that the pilot and the navigator, having been flung through the Plexiglas nose on impact, had suffered more grievous hurts.

The three most mobile having settled somewhat, and with two dinghies impressed into service to shelter the pilot and navigator from the elements, Second Lieutenant Parks set off into the drizzly darkness to seek aid. Initially he trekked downhill along the debris trail, then followed a stream until he eventually saw an unshielded light: although the European War had only a month to run, and although restrictions had been gradually lifted over the last year or so, these High-Peak epics are studded with this fine disregard for blackout regulations which, on occasion – as here – guided survivors to safety.

Brow Grain Cottage

The co-pilot had actually come down between Brow Grain Hill and Bracken Hill, to the north-east of the crash site, and found succour at Brow Grain Cottage, then a Water Board property, where the resident waterman, Mr Tasker, raised the alarm.

The first band of rescuers brought in the radio operator and the flight engineer but were loth to move the pilot and navigator until a doctor had pronounced upon them; yet setting out following a doctor's arrival, and supplemented by two stretcher parties, the rescuers themselves ran into difficulties. Seeing none of the anticipated guidance flares, they got disorientated in a thickening mist and eventually had to return to Brow Grain Cottage. Indeed, conditions had worsened so much that it then took Mr Tasker himself, supported by his dog, one and a half hours to lead them to the site. Even then the ordeal was not over for either rescued or rescuers, for the stretcher teams disagreed over the return routing, each eventually going its own way. Both, however, arrived back safely.

Shortly after dawn a salvage team arrived, and after specialists had located the then-secret Norden bombsight, they proceeded to dispose of, burn, and bury most of the wreckage.

The then-secret Norden Bombsight

The inquiry into the crash ruled that it had been caused by the pilot persisting in trying to maintain visual-contact flight in unsuitable weather conditions when lost over unknown, high-level terrain. Only, as the co-pilot had actually been at the controls when the accident occurred, he – and not the aircraft commander – was the pilot charged with the accident!

Tragically, both First Lieutenant Johnson and Second Lieutenant Vukelic had suffered broken spines and were subsequently confined to wheelchairs. Indeed, when First Lieutenant Johnson died in 1961 it was held to be a direct result of the spinal injury received that night.

Mrs Joyce Casseli, of Meltham – ten-year-old Joyce Hooley in 1945 – remembered the excitement the crash caused locally. 'At the time', she recalled, 'we lived in Marsden, and after the first few days, when nobody was allowed near – because of the danger, or secrecy, perhaps – it proved a great draw. And not only for us children, so grown-ups too used to bring souvenirs down: metal, perspex and the like. But my mother refused to have anything from the plane in the house. So I didn't take anything.' Pressed about the perspex, Joyce smiled. 'I did have a perspex brooch during the war – but it wasn't from there …'

Perspex – or its kindred thermoplastic – had rather more significance for the regular bombardier of the crew, Second Lieutenant Dick Kinder, who had been stood down for the ill-fated flight. Later the erstwhile bombardier made a return visit for the launch of the *Dark Peak Aircraft Wrecks* (Ron Collier) in the 1980s where he told Peak Park Ranger Peter Jackson that had he been aboard and at his station he too would almost certainly have been thrown through the Plexiglas and seriously injured.

Former bombardier Dick Kinder, 1988

Notwithstanding the diligence of the salvage party in burying the debris, much re-emerged over the years. Consequently, being in a relatively remote spot, and even in the brightest of weather vividly reflecting the difficulties facing both the shocked co-pilot and the rescue teams who had to traverse the moor on a rainy, mist-laden night, the crash site still displayed a substantial amount of surface debris in 2013.

Debris, 2013

VISITING THE SITE

Convenient lay-by parking for two cars can be found on the road to the south-west of Meltham at SE 08008 08743, 433 metres. From the outset this is an unashamed, off-path site, three-quarters of a moorland mile from the road. And yet, in the main, visiting it is not that laborious an undertaking. The outbound walk will take something like thirty minutes, the foray affording splendid landscape views both going and coming. The initial 300 yard stretch to gain the West Nab Ridge from the roadside requires negotiating malevolently unpleasant hummock grass but progress becomes easier as the ridge is reached. At that juncture it is probably worthwhile angling westwards to the trig column before setting course downslope across heather and coarse grasses for the Wicken Stones group, 700 yards from the ridge. The crash site lies 425 yards beyond the Stones and comprises a burnt patch with metal shards and a substantial main-debris group, both in black peat among broken ground.

In 2013 the site lay just within the proscribed fall-of-shot safety area of the Deer Hill Shooting Range, which may not be shown on earlier map issues. However, although the butts are some 1.1 miles (1.8 km) distant from the red and white boundary markers, best not quibble with possibly-flying lead, and certainly, red flags are always to be respected.

What no walker should miss before leaving the West Nab area are the various singularly-shaped and naturally-holed rocks.

Dovestone Reservoir Area

4. Consolidated Vultee PB4Y-1 Liberator 63934
Broken Ground, east of Mossley

SE 00930 01562 431 m (See below for the coordinates of other debris)
Unit and Station: United States Navy, VB110 Bombing Squadron, AAF173 (RAF Dunkeswell), north-east of Exeter
Date: 18 December 1943
Occupants: one passenger, ten crew, most Naval Reserve. All successfully parachuted, five suffering minor injuries:

- Lieutenant George H. Charno, Jr, pilot
- Lieutenant Junior Grade Robert G. Wissman, co-pilot, injured
- Ensign Cecil R. Colyer, navigator, injured
- Aviation Chief Radioman (ACRM 1) Boyd S. Barber, US Navy, injured, with shock
- Aviation Radioman (ARM 3) Warren W. Olson, radio operator
- Aviation Ordnanceman (AOM) Walter O. Levering, weapons
- Aviation Machinist's Mate (AMM 3) Douglas S. Peterson, radio operator
- Aviation Machinist's Mate (AMM 3) Archie P. Oliver, engineer, injured
- Seaman 2nd Class Dewey M. Clark, gunner
- Seaman 2nd Class Winston C. Ketchem, gunner
- Seaman 2nd Class William J. Clayton, ground crewman, passenger, broken ribs

Consolidated-Vultee PB4Y Liberator

In early 1943 RAF Dunkeswell hosted three American squadrons operating the maritime variant of the Liberator known as the PB4Y-1 – PB denoting Patrol Bomber. Among them was VB110 Bombing Squadron – 'V' denoting aeroplane; 'B', bomber –, one of whose aircraft was to be abandoned by its crew in the vicinity of the Wash and to come down in the High Peak area near Mossley.

This was PB4Y 63934 in which Lieutenant George Charno and his predominantly United States Naval Reserve crew were tasked to carry out an anti-submarine patrol in the Biscay area. They had left RAF Dunkeswell, to the north-east of Exeter, at 0700 hours on 18 December 1943, having been briefed to expect an early recall due to an anticipated deterioration in the United Kingdom weather. The recall came at 1100 hours after they had completed just a single radar sweep of their patrol area, high winds, turbulence, constant rain, and a solid 400-foot cloud base having nullified a visual-contact search. The recall order required them to arrive back at their Dunkeswell base by 1700 hours and must have been received in the spirit of a half-holiday award, letting them off, as it promised to, with just a twelve-hour flight.

Lieutenant Charno's established crew of specialists were accustomed to co-operating together on long-range maritime operations that invariably called for many hours of seemingly unproductive – and therefore frustrating – patrolling, often enough to be flown at low level and in such characteristically appalling weather conditions as those they were returning from. Which was just as well, for the British weather was to take no account of any holiday expectations; on the contrary, it was to set about taxing them to the very limit of their combined forbearance.

A crew of specialists ...
En route to the UK, Meeks Field, Iceland, 1 October 1943

Left to right, standing: Lieutenant Junior Grade Robert G. Wissman, co-pilot; Ensign Cecil R. Colyer, navigator; Lieutenant George H. Charno, Jr, pilot; Aviation Ordnanceman (AOM) Walter O. Levering, weapons; Aviation Machinist's Mate (AMM 3) Douglas S. Peterson, radio operator; not in crash crew; Aviation Radioman (ARM 3) Warren W. Olson, radio operator. Kneeling, first two not in crash crew; Seaman 2nd Class William J. Clayton, ground crewman, passenger; Seaman 2nd Class Dewey M. Clark, gunner. (Not present on the Atlantic ferry flight, were: Aviation Chief Radioman (ACRM 1) Boyd S. Barber; Aviation Machinist's Mate Archie P. Oliver, engineer; Seaman 2nd Class Winston C. Ketchem, gunner). **Courtesy Mr George Charno, via David W. Earl**

At first all went to order, and making use of a timely fix obtained by one of their W/T (wireless telegraphy: morse) operators, they accomplished a landfall at Bude, on the North Cornish coast, at 1600 hours, allowing them to penetrate inland while keeping visual contact below cloud at just 500 feet above ground level. The overland weather deterioration, however, had set in earlier than expected, and on contacting No. 19 Group, RAF, the controlling authority, and having already passed overhead the first possible bad-weather bolt hole – RAF Winkleigh, to the north-west of Exeter –, they were ordered to overfly their Dunkeswell base and divert to RAF Beaulieu, in the New Forest, to the west of Southampton.

Lieutenant Charno would later record that, having looked down at both Winkleigh and Dunkeswell in passing, he could still have made a safe landing at either despite conditions already being rendered marginal by low ceiling, reduced visibility in drizzle, and high winds. As it was, however, he was obliged to trust to Group's having its paternal eye on some bigger picture, and obediently held course for Beaulieu.

Navigation was aided by a series of headings obtained by W/T, despite the fact that with the manual direction-finding of the day, and the poor reception occasioned by heavy static on this particular late afternoon, such vital bearings, spelled out in morse, often took five minutes to arrive on the navigator's table. But even as they neared Beaulieu the poor visibility was exacerbated by heavy rain, forcing Lieutenant Charno to climb to 1,500 feet and revert to flight on instruments alone.

The initial approach, consequently, embarked upon with the aim of making visual contact with Beaulieu, saw them letting down on an easterly heading-to-steer obtained by W/T. They actually broke cloud at some 700 feet, but although lookouts were positioned at every hatch, supplementing the eyes in the cockpit, they saw no sign of the airfield; indeed, minutes later, another bearing showed that they had passed it by. They duly commenced a westerly turn to take them back to the airfield area but as they did so the nearby barrage-balloon defences of Southampton were seen rearing to 5,000 feet above them. Prudent avoidance procedure called for an immediate southerly turn, notwithstanding which, moments later, they began receiving balloon-hazard radio signals. Happily, being in visual contact with the surface as these warnings sounded, they were able to discount them as spurious, and some time later were able to fix themselves off the coast near Portsmouth, to the east of Southampton.

With the crew now positive of their position the co-pilot, Lieutenant Robert Wissman, used the topographical chart to map-read them to the mouth of the Beaulieu River, from which there was every chance of their making a successful visual approach. By now, however, they were up against rapidly deteriorating visibility and although Lieutenant Charno managed to make fleeting radio telephony (R/T: voice) contact with Beaulieu and requested full airfield lighting to assist them in locating the field, he was told that the lights had been fully on from the outset. At this crucial moment a hazard-warning-ahead advisory from the W/T operator necessitated a ninety-degree heading change, the attendant climb to a recommended 1,700 feet safe height taking them, willy-nilly, back into the turbulent overcast.

By then it was 1745 hours, December's daylight had long waned, the high winds and gusty conditions were making flight on instruments difficult, and with heavy rain now falling it became evident that contact flying, and continuing to attempt to make visual approaches without ground assistance, was no longer tenable. Nor was their own airborne radar able to assist in conditions so bumpy, accordingly, Lieutenant Charno had the radioman currently at the wireless operator's station, Aviation Radioman Boyd Barber, call for a formal 'Controlled Descent Through Cloud' (CDTC).

In later years, when voice communication and automatic direction-finding would provide instantaneous headings to steer, the CDTC – or to use the handier, brevity-code terminology, the QGH – became the standard non-radar method of safely descending cloud-thwarted aircraft. At this period, however, when it depended upon morse code and manual direction-finding, it was a very protracted procedure. Just the same it was a relatively sure method of penetrating through to any reasonable cloud base, the ground controller routing the machine to clear all obstructions and high terrain. On this occasion, though, Lieutenant Charno, with a declared three hours of fuel still on board, was asked to hold off, as other, lower-endurance, aircraft were also endeavouring to make approaches.

Lieutenant Charno dutifully positioned himself to the north of Beaulieu, maintaining his 1,700 feet until the time came when those aircraft had completed their approaches and he was called back to commence his own let-down. Only the moment he settled onto the heading passed to home him to the overhead, balloon-hazard signals forced him to turn aside. Nor, for fear of collision in cloud with other still-dwelling aircraft, could he afford to climb above the hazard signals; had he been able to do so he would have held his extra height until control had ascertained that he was safely overhead Beaulieu. Except that, in mid-dilemma, the Liberator's main radio equipment broke down altogether.

In this extremity, cut off from any form of ground control, no matter how tenuous, flying through thick, turbulent cloud in an airspace congested not only with unseen aircraft milling about to no set pattern (in those days), but with balloon cables hungry for trade, whether enemy or Allied, Lieutenant Charno initiated the first of a series of calls to the 'Darky' emergency-homing service on his limited-range voice radio. All he received, however, was one unintelligible response, after which nothing more was heard despite attempts which were continued throughout the remainder of the flight.

He also had the 'Identification Friend or Foe' (IFF) equipment turned to 'Emergency', although this would have been more to conform with signals procedures rather than in expectation of ground radar stations actually seeing the singular alerting code and organising a shepherd aircraft to first locate him, and then guide him to a more suitable airfield. Just the same, at 1830 hours, it did seem as if Lieutenant Charno's crew had been granted a reprieve, for at this stage W/T contact with Beaulieu was regained, and another controlled descent begun. In the course of this, however, balloon hazard warnings started to come in once again, but this time Lieutenant Charno was satisfied that he was far enough north-west of Beaulieu to ignore them, and carried on descending. At which juncture the W/T finally cut out altogether, never to be restored.

Pragmatically accepting that they had now been irretrievably cast upon their own resources, Lieutenant Charno continued his descent on the last received safe heading, with all aboard straining to sight either airfield lights or cloud-base-locating searchlights. Only nothing relieved the opacity as they nosed down from the cloud rack. But not long afterwards flares were seen; indeed, on two occasions. Yet, although the aircraft was immediately turned towards them, the crew then found only darkness. Anticipation heightened to eagerness just a little later when they all thought they had finally seen an airfield and even a flarepath, but after several low orbits had been made the navigator, Ensign Cecil Colyer, identified the hoped-for flarepath as nothing but the dimmed headlights of a convoy of lorries.

Clearly there was nothing to be achieved by continuing to randomly hunt about at hazardously low level in such poor visibility, and so Lieutenant Charno commenced a spiral climb above this provenly safe area, and at 5,000 feet set a northerly heading. Their best hope now, it seemed evident, was to head towards the Midlands, an area where airfields abounded: not for nothing was wartime Britain talked of as an aircraft carrier moored off Europe.

Lieutenant Charno's was a reasoned course of action, yet as they progressed northwards, over what they discovered to be persistently unbroken cloud above a blacked-out land, hopes of finding any useful clearance began to fade, and as time dragged on and the fuel gauges began demanding notice, it became clear that the aircraft might well have to be abandoned. There was at least one other alternative, of course, that of descending blind through cloud and hoping to emerge into clear air before hitting the ground; to his further credit Lieutenant Charno discounted this course out of hand.

Then again, when he purposefully broached the subject of abandoning by parachute, one crew member, no doubt impelled by the universal reluctance of aircrew to leave an aircraft by any other means than down its steps, did suggest that they might turn towards the sea – whether east or west did not signify, with Britain not being that wide – and put the aircraft onto the water. But it was a suggestion only tentatively made, for nobody on board had any illusions regarding the Liberator's ditching characteristics: parachutes it would have to be. Therefore, as yet more time passed, and still no gaps were seen in the cloud below, so preparations were set in hand.

Radar Operator Douglas Peterson busied himself in ensuring that the radar dome was fully retracted and in destroying the still-secret components; Aviation Ordnanceman Warren Olson double-checked that his charges – mines and the very secret acoustic torpedoes – were, indeed, unarmed; and Aviation Radioman Boyd Barber, at the W/T set, persisted until the last in tapping away at his morse key, hoping that transmissions, at least, might be getting through, dead though reception was. But finally, with only an estimated fifteen minutes' fuel left in his tanks, Lieutenant Charno set the auto pilot to head just north of west, opened the bomb-bay doors – the safest parachuting exit –, and ordered the crew to jump.

The evacuation went like the pre-ordained drill, except that (as former-Aviation Radioman Douglas Peterson would recall in a 1995 letter) Aviation Ordnanceman Orville Levering snagged his ripcord handle on a projection, so that when his turn came he had to jump with his part-opened canopy hugged in his arms. Lieutenant Charno, leaving the auto-pilot engaged, waited until the last of his crew, co-pilot Lieutenant Wissman, was clear, and then followed in his wake.

The abandonment was highly successful, and although there were a few superficial contusions, and a broken rib or two on landing, this was hardly surprising with a surface wind logged at forty-eight miles an hour and using parachutes of a type which, for many years afterwards, limited even paratroop training drops to a maximum surface wind strength of ten miles an hour.

In his letter Mr Peterson described his own bale-out experience. 'I pulled the rip cord,' he wrote, 'and when the chute opened it knocked the wind out of me … I stopped and my flight boots kept right on going, so I landed in my socks. Being it was a blackout I didn't even see the ground when I hit it, a plowed and muddy field. I couldn't spill the [twenty-eight-foot diameter] chute and was dragged a couple hundred feet before it spilled over a hedgerow.' Gathering his parachute he then walked some quarter of a mile to a house. 'The man let me in (I was covered in mud) and his wife laid a bunch of newspapers on the floor and I peeled the mud off and got out of my mae west and chute harness.' The man provided him with a pair of old shoes, and having taken him to the local pub, where he phoned his position through to base, took him back to the house where 'his wife made some bacon and eggs (which you didn't see much) and later a couple of bobbies came and took me to Boston (they had picked up 11 when I got there), and then to an RAF airfield where we had physicals. Next day we went to London and next day a Catalina flew us all back to base.'

As the crew had variously discovered, a strong south-westerly wind had acted upon them throughout their northerly passage, so that, when they abandoned, they had been in the vicinity of the Wash, on the East Coast. But, while, in retrospect, it might seem that Lieutenant Charno would have been better advised to turn the aircraft onto an easterly heading for abandoning (rather then one just north of west), this would be to take unfair advantage of hindsight, particularly with the British Isles being such a deceptive shape. (For example, steering northwards from Liverpool, does Edinburgh lie to the east or the west?) After all, having set a northerly course from the New Forest area, Lieutenant Charno might reasonably have expected to be abandoning in the Midlands, equally close to either coast. As for the ordnance left on board – the mines and the torpedoes – not having been armed, these presented no more of a threat than materiel of that nature ever does.

Left to its own devices, the machine, with its automatic pilot engaged and trimmed to straight flight – if commencing a steady descent once Lieutenant Charno had vacated – and with little fuel registering on the gauges, flew on westwards, heading, as it transpired, directly for the Ashton-under-Lyne area of Manchester. It had already reached a concerningly low altitude by the time it was seen over the Tame Valley. But at that juncture – it has to be assumed – a starboard engine ran out of fuel and cut, for when the Liberator was next seen, further north, over Mossley, it was heading eastwards, the drag of the windmilling propeller evidently having pulled it into a wide curve to the right. Just a short while later, and providentially after clearing the built-up areas, it had descended so far that it struck the top of the barren, peat-surfaced plateau of Broken Ground at 1,400 feet above sea level. There was no fire on impact, nor did the ordnance explode.

The United States Navy's investigating board found that the pivotal communications failure was due to no apparently remediable cause, and consequently recorded the accident under the miscellaneous category: 10% attributable to radio failure, and 80% to weather.

Following this, Lieutenant Charno received a well-merited commendation for, 'Taking correct and decisive action in an emergency and for the obvious good discipline of the crew'. Obvious, that is, in the sense that their good discipline illumined the whole episode. Additionally, what has to be reiterated is that here is one captain who, despite having seemingly pulled out all the stops in his protracted efforts to save his aircraft, did not then make the mistake made by so many others, that of fatally hazarding his crew by descending blindly below cloud once they were no longer receiving radio-navigational assistance and had become hopelessly lost!

The present 'aviator's-view' account having very properly highlighted the exemplary conduct of each member of Lieutenant Charno's crew (other, 'enthusiast' accounts haven't done so), it might be politic to declare the sources used in its compilation. These comprise the official statement submitted by Lieutenant Charno to the United States Navy's investigating board (the endearingly styled 'Trouble Board'); the Naval Accident Report, Form 339, entitled 'Aircraft Trouble Report'; two letters written by the former-Lieutenant Charno in August and October 1998 respectively; and the letter, previously referred to, written by former-Aviation Radioman Douglas S. Peterson. All these documents were supplied by the Hell on High Ground series author Mr David W. Earl (see Selected References) together with his permission to use them here.

GEORGE H. CHARNO, JR.
121 WEST 48TH ST.
KANSAS CITY, MO 64112
Aug. 7, 1998

He did the create the conversations I referred to previously.
They never occurred. He apparently had access to the accident
report I filed and from it extrapolated inaccurately, although
of no particular moment in the course of history. For example,
he describes how my copilot took over the controls and attempted
to fly us to the field at Beaulieu. I wrote that when we saw the
Isle of Wight, he tried to navigate us to the field by "pilotage."
That word means using a map and identifying landmarks by sight as
compared to navigating by radio aids or some other way. It
doen't mean taking over the controls. I would agree that this is
nit-picking but I thought I would answer your question. The
conversation I best recall was when I told the crew we needed
to bail out, one of them asked me on the intercom if we could'nt
fly out to sea and ditch the plane instead of parachuting. I had
little difficulty in rejecting this as an alternative.

Lieutenant Charno's 1998 Letter

Regrettably, in 1982, a journalistically-styled account was published which presented this estimable crew in an altogether less favourable light. This centred upon the passage, 'Now just leave it to me!' Snapped [co-pilot] Wissman determinedly as he took over the controls' (*Dark Peak Aircraft Wrecks, 2*, page 67, see Selected References). In glaring contrast, the documents cited above prove that portrayal to have misinterpreted salient facts, thereby doing the crew a disservice that cannot sit easily with anyone who has ever flown professionally, whether Service or Civil; be it as a pilot, or as the member of an aircrew.

> The write up about us bailing out was fairly accurate except the writer had a vivid imagination. I was the radioman plus radar on the flight. The air was toorough the radar was useless so I cranked it up (manually), as it was where the bottom turret would normally be and it sutck out quite a bit, and I didn't want that hanging down in case we had to leave the aircraft. There were two radiomen on the crew, one of us was on radar and the other on the radio, we took turns at operating each position. With the problems with the radio, which was not uncommon, my trying to get soemthing to work was not bordring on panic, but on frustration. Orville Levering, one of the mechs, did not pull the rip cord handle as the article states but it got caught on one of the nandles of the radar and it popped the chute. He held it in his arms and when he was clear of the aircraft he let go and it opened.

Radioman Peterson's 1995 letter

Certainly it was a portrayal refuted by both former-Lieutenant Charno and by former-Aviation Radioman Peterson; not that either, as generous American gentlemen, was anything but indulgent. Mr Peterson merely allowed that 'the writer had a vivid imagination'. The former-Lieutenant Charno, for his part, benignly saw the over-excitable extravagances as 'the figment of someone's imagination', and attributed the most glaring to the writer's having 'extrapolated inaccurately, although of no particular moment in the course of history'. But he especially singled out the compiler's evident misinterpretation of the word 'pilotage', which Lieutenant Charno had used in his 1943 report. For far from meaning that the co-pilot suddenly seized control, it merely means to navigate by map reading.

N. Act. 329
(Revised Apr. 1942)

AIRCRAFT TROUBLE REPORT

(See BuAero Circular Letter No. 24-41 for detailed instructions in making out this Report)

Unit to which aircraft assigned.........Bombing Squadron 110................................ A. T. R. Serial No. ....
The Trouble Board met (place) RAF Sta Dunkeswell.; (date) 22 December 1943 ; and found the following to be true:
Accident (place)............Devon England. ; (date) 18 December 1943 ; (hour) Unknown
Time in flight until occurrence of trouble near Manchester, England.   Purpose of flight: A/S Patrol

		AIRCRAFT	ENGINE	ENGINE	ENGINE	ENGINE

STATEMENT OF LT.(JG) G.H. GHARNO OF FLIGHT 18 DECEMBER 1943
110-B-2, BUREAU NO. 63934

Aircraft Trouble Report

Regarding the Liberator's impact site, veteran researcher Mr John Ownsworth remembered that the scrap dealer who recovered the wreckage utilised sections of it to fence off his lot. Even so, three engines (no researcher seems to know anything of the fourth engine) and the main-undercarriage members remained on the surface for many years. Then, in 2002, in a reciprocal arrangement with the moor's gamekeeper, some components were removed while the other large items were buried, deliberately at some remove. This meant that very little surface evidence was left, just a minuscule pool of collected debris and a myriad scraps of metal littering a wide area of the pitch-black peat.

Author David W. Earl at the impact site, 2010

VISITING THE SITE

Walkers examine debris

The most likely starting point for visiting this site has to be from the Pay and Display car park at Dovestone Reservoir. This is accessed from Bank Lane, which leads off the A635 Holmfirth Road at SE 00765 03976. It should be noted, however, that when approaching from the east the turn into Bank Lane is so acute that road signs oblige vehicles to continue to the next roundabout, then turn back. Having complied, and safely parked, two ways offer themselves to the site.

The first, both the most direct, and certainly the most laborious, heads west along Bradbury's Lane to the footpath opposite the row of cottages at SE 00856 03467, 211 metres. The footpath leads upwards, crossing two paths, the second being Intake Lane – the old Chew Reservoir construction-railway route, now become the Oldham Way. From here the route continues directly uphill on 220°M, the unremitting 640 yard off-path slog to the 460 metre Alphin Pike trig column (SE 00299 02822) taking of the order of an hour. From there the main crash-site area lies some 0.87 miles (1.5 km) distant on a heading of 157°M. The intervening Broken Ground, however, affords relatively easy walking, largely across black peat cut with always manageable groughs and, increasingly, over stretches of regenerated heather.

Researcher and aviation artist Alan Jones with metal detector but also the steel probe, for many years his sole aid in detecting buried debris

A more evenly paced ascent is to follow the road past the sailing club to just short of the Chew Brook Bridge before taking the southerly footpath up through the woods to climb the left-hand side of the not-that-demanding Rams Clough. On reaching Hoarstone Edge (at SE 01743 02339) an off-path heading of 221°M will lead, over pleasantly grough-bisected peat, to the site in 0.71 miles (1.15 km).

Other walkers may decide to leave Intake Lane shortly after passing above the Kinder Intake gamekeeper's cottage and climb the gully, known locally as Green Clough, entering at SE 01465 02884 and 277 metres. This route passes (or did in 2013) one of the undercarriage frames of Dakota G-AHCY (see below) and may be as conveniently made by the stream bed as the slopes. Then, once the Hoarstone Edge is reached, at SE 01505 02422, a heading of 209°M over undulating peaty moorland will lead to the Liberator impact site after 0.65 of a mile (1.05 km). As it happens, after 800 yards the track passes close to the spurious site associated with a Hurricane crash (see Sites With No Surface Debris, Section 10, below).

Perhaps the most straightforward way of reaching the Liberator site, however, is to ascend from Carrbrook, south-east of Mossley, where opportunity car parking is available at SD 98933 01113 at 197 metres. After that, a well defined route, part quarry trail, part walker's track, leads up to the crash-site area on Broken Ground and thence to Hoarstone Edge.

The coordinates for the Liberator crash site, as given (SE 00930 01562 431 m), are those of the location where Mr Alan Jones and Mr David W. Earl remember clambering on the main wreckage pile. Beyond that, the area abounds with small surface debris which, from time to time, may be found gathered in various circlets of rocks. In the 1970s the local gamekeeper dissuaded visitors, but Mr Jones brokered an agreement by which certain items might be retrieved on condition that he buried others. By 2013 some of these had been unearthed, so that an undercarriage section lay on the surface at SE 00873 01591, at 431 metres, while another lay concealed at SE 00820 01667, at 437 metres, as did an engine at SE 00838 01628, at 437 metres. Another engine, which was rolled 460 yards downhill in an unrelated and never renewed bid at retrieval, was rediscovered at SE 00508 01578, at 380 metres.

For other local-area sites, a heading of 030°M for 0.69 miles (1.1 km) leads to Wimberry Stones on the Hoarstone Edge and the crash site of Dakota G-AHCY (see below). From there, continuing easterly along the fine Hoarstone Edge rim path for a mile and a half, leads to Chew Reservoir and the nearby site of DH82A Tiger Moth T6464 (see below).

Though the view from Hoarstone Edge towards Dovestone Reservoir is spectacular, the many names and initials spelled out in tiny rocks on the peat edges above Wimberry Stones are well worth a passing look.

As for bad-weather descent routes from Broken Ground, that from Carrbrook can be reversed, utilising Far Harehill Clough to pick up a path; while the swiftest safe descent to Dovestone Reservoir can be made from the rim path at Wimberry Stones, using either the previously mentioned Green Gully or the less demanding (below the initial stage) Rams Clough.

From the main Liberator site, the possible crash site of a Spitfire, on Irontongue Hill (see Sites With No Surface Debris, Section 17), lies a scenic 0.73 miles distant on a heading of 151°M.

5. Douglas Dakota G-AHCY
Wimberry Stones Brow, Chew Valley

SE 01556 02451 413 m, impact site
SE 01494 02686 325 m, undercarriage member
Operator: British European Airways (BEA)
Date 19 April 1949
Occupants: three crew and twenty-one passengers died, eight survived.
These died:

- Captain Frank Whartley Pinkerton
- First Officer George Holt
- Radio Officer Richard Willis Haig

Mrs Edith Holt Barclay, Miss Jean Barclay, Mr Willie Ashton, Mrs Margery Davies, Mr Hubert Stanley Lea, Mr Cyril Beenstock, Miss Dorothy May Brimelow, Mr Derek Harry Clarke, Master Roger Alan Evans, Miss Bridget Ann Farrell, Mr George Stephen Gisby, Miss Ivy Gwendoline Jones, Mrs Elizabeth Schofield, Mrs Beatrice Sydall, Mrs Edna Vickery, Master David Vickery, Mrs Joan Prestwich, Mr Henry Bryce Prestwich, Miss Elizabeth Anne Prestwich, Miss Jane Caroline Prestwich, Mrs Sarah Marguerite Baird.

These passengers, though injured, survived:
Mr Robert F. Ashton, Mr Horace Evans, Mrs Ruth Evans, Master Stephen Evans, Miss Kathleen McMahon, Master Michael Prestwich, Mr Arthur Frank Vickery, Mr Christopher Watt.

Douglas Dakota of British European Airways

The loss of twenty-four lives on 19 April 1949, when BEA Dakota G-AHCY crashed on the heights of the Chew Valley, just over fifteen miles north-east of Manchester Airport, was found to be caused by the failure of Captain Pinkerton and his crew to correctly establish their position on the radio beam designed to get them down safely through cloud. It might be apposite, therefore, to consider the bad-weather aid-to-landing system in use in 1949.

In essence, the main airfield beacon of the Standard Beam Approach System (SBA) was situated at the far end of the runway from the touchdown point and transmitted a thirty-mile-long, very narrow radio beam down the extended centre-line of the runway. This told a pilot receiving the aural 'on-the-beam' signal that he was somewhere along the projected centre-line of the runway.

To furnish an exact location *along* the beam, an 'outer marker' radio beacon was sited at – in Manchester's case – some two miles from touchdown. This sent a coded signal vertically upwards to tell an inbound pilot that he had that far to go and should commence his final descent to land. There was also an 'inner marker', sited some 150 yards from touchdown.

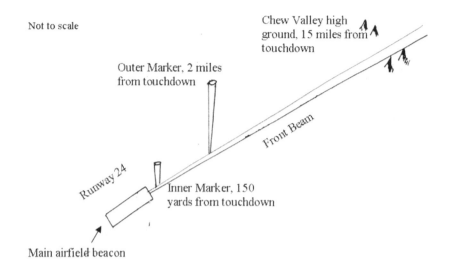

Essential elements of the Manchester Standard Beam Approach System (SBA), 1949

Such marker-beacon signals, however, were not designed to cause the needle of a radio compass to point towards them. This meant that, in order to positively ascertain that he was over the airfield before establishing himself on the beam, a pilot would normally have to home to a dedicated airfield beacon to which the needle did point. G-AHCY had a radio compass for this purpose, but at that time Manchester had no such beacon. The standard starting procedure, therefore, was to navigate to the SBA's main airfield beacon and take advantage of the sudden loss of signal – the cone of silence – experienced when passing directly over it. Now confident that he was over Manchester, the pilot would then use the beam to suitably distance himself beyond the outer marker.

On the other hand, it was perfectly permissible to navigate directly to the outer marker by independent means. And this, as the surviving aircraft navigational and radio logs told the inquiry, was the course of action the captain had decided upon.

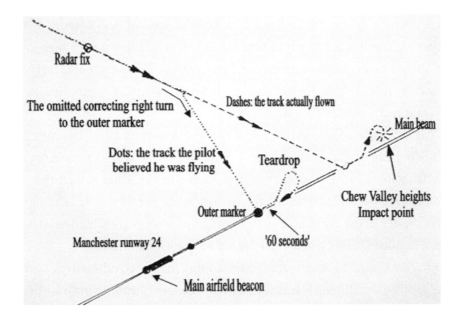

Tracks pertinent to the crash of G-AHCY

Of critical importance to the investigation, the navigation log showed that G-AHCY, inbound from Belfast, had approached the area on a reasonable heading for the airfield, that in order to refine his heading, Captain Pinkerton had obtained a radar fix. As plotted, this had indicated that he was presently heading somewhat wide of both airfield beacon and outer marker, indeed, aiming towards the high ground of the Chew Valley. The correction required – and logged as having been made by the first officer! – was a change of heading to the right. As the investigators appreciated, the calculated alteration would not have taken the aircraft over the airfield beacon but would have brought it – very usefully – onto the front beam near the outer marker. Except that despite the log entry, Captain Pinkerton never did make that vital correcting turn!

Trying to determine why the turn was never made would engage the air accident investigators in much deliberation. One of the factors to be considered, of course, was the dependability of the captain. Yet here, as with the technical equipment concerned, it was difficult to find fault: an ex-wartime bomber pilot who had successfully evaded capture after being shot down, Captain Pinkerton had a healthy total of 3,391 hours' flying experience and was known to first officers who had flown with him to be an operator who adhered to standard procedures. The inescapable fact was, however, that despite the telling fix obtained, G-AHCY continued to be flown directly towards the high ground.

It had to be concluded that, in Captain Pinkerton's mind, the turn had actually been made, leaving him convinced that he would now intercept the front beam in the vicinity of the outer marker. After which the rest would have been plain sailing, for he had made nearly ninety landings at Manchester in the previous two years, a fair proportion of which must have been in poor visibility, and with the aid of its beam approach.

What Captain Pinkerton envisaged doing from then on – as reflected by the air-traffic radio log – was to maintain the 'new' heading until he heard the coding of the outer marker. The procedure would then require him to turn smartly left and fly the beam *away* from the runway for a timed sixty seconds. With that time up he would then fly a stylised teardrop-shaped 'procedural turn' designed to bring him back on to the beam again, but inbound now, towards the runway, with the outer marker ahead, dutifully waiting to tell him when to commence his final approach from his cleared 1,500 feet.

Except that, as Captain Pinkerton was never to know, when he first intercepted the beam – and advised Manchester that he had done so – he was nowhere near the outer marker, but some eleven miles downwind from it. In his own mind, however, although he could not hear the coding, he would have 'known' that he was very close to its overhead. So he turned anyway, timed his sixty seconds away from the airfield, then embarked upon the teardrop-shaped 'procedural turn': first left, spacing him from the beam, then a long, steady, partly descending right turn all the way around, to gradually establish on the beam inbound. Only, in reality, he was flying out this procedure with reference to a phantom marker. And it was in the course of this protracted right-hand turn that he flew his passengers and crew into the only too real 1,500-foot elevation of Wimberry Stones Brow, fifteen miles from the runway.

As it happened, the last few moments of the flight had been seen, so that testifying witnesses were able to tell the inquiry that the aircraft had been turning, or completing a turn, in a wheels-down configuration. The investigators, therefore, had been able to conclude that, 'probably during the procedure turn', the aircraft had been descended some 350 feet (from the initial 1,500 feet) before crashing.

Of more immediate significance, because the crash had been seen, rescuers reached the scene with surprising speed and were able to carry eight survivors to safety, saving at least one from the encroaching flames. Nothing could be done, however, for the other twenty-one passengers, for Captain Pinkerton, or for his crew.

Contemporary press photo of the crash scene

Contemporary photographs of the scene show rescuers swarming on the steep, debris-scattered slopes of the clough – unnamed on maps, but known to keepers as Green Clough – where the aircraft impacted. For many years, though, there has been nothing to show of the tragedy enacted above this scenically-rich ravine. Yet the site is more remote than others nearby where surface debris still remained from much smaller aeroplanes. The conclusion to be drawn being that, even then, back in 1949, no civil company wanted to perpetuate its mistakes, but rather took pains to ensure that not a trace was left.

Mr James Bradbury, gamekeeper and sheep farmer, of the gamekeeper's cottage at Kinder Intake, below the clough, was able to throw some light on the actual clearance. 'It was RAF, or anyway, aeroplane men who actually did the clearing: and they hardly left anything. The big stuff they dragged down to the fields where it was handed over to Fred Shackleton, who had a Fergie tractor.' He smiled. 'Fred was in farming, not scrap dealing, but he was a larger-than-life character and'd never miss a trick if there was money in it.'

Significantly – in considering locating crash sites from official records – the slopes were left so bare of debris that without photographic and witness evidence, positively identifying the impact area would have been difficult. This was because the official accident report has the crash occurring at 53°31′00″N 01°58′30″W (which converts to SE 01750 02220, or just above Rams Clough). The actual impact point, however, is 330 yards distant, beyond the singularly shaped Wimberry Stones (popularly, Indian's Head) on the slopes of the adjoining Unnamed, or Green Clough to the west.

The location, above the crash site, recorded in the official report

It is clear therefore, that the compilers of this civil report – like the compilers of so many Service crash reports – saw no need to be any more precise. This is borne out by the fact that the elevation of the location given is 1,500 feet rather than the 'between 1,250 and 1,400 feet' impact elevation of their report.

Just the same, despite the wealth of photographic evidence showing the impact site, it was particularly gratifying when researching this site in 2005, to find a tiny fragment of molten aluminium, a fragment secreted in situ to continue to bear mute witness.

The sole fragment found at the impact point, since secreted in situ

Certainly, in 2013, there was just one other long-term survivor in the shape of an undercarriage frame lying in the lower reaches of Green Clough.

An undercarriage frame, 2013

And as a footnote, poignant rather than ironic, Captain Pinkerton had been a keen walker, and the Chew Valley, understandably, one of his favourite haunts.

VISITING THE SITE

A distant view of the sites

Accessing Dovestone Reservoir and its car park is detailed in Section 4. Having parked, the most popular way of visiting the Dakota crash site, and the least laborious – say local keepers –, is to take the footpath leading past the sailing club to a point just short of the Chew Brook bridge. From here a southerly footpath runs up the left-hand side of Rams Clough and, after a steady climb of some twenty minutes, leads to the dramatically sculptured Wimberry Stones and the virtual plateau of Wimberry Moss. Other walkers may well decide upon their own routings from the map, particularly those utilising Intake Lane – the Oldham Way – to ascend the unnamed 'Green' gully which issues at SE 01465 02884, 277 metres and harbours the previously mentioned undercarriage member at SE 01494 02686, 325 metres (certainly, until 2013). Continuing upwards, it is a matter of choice whether to use the shoulder of the gully or the easily-stepped rock ladder afforded by the stream, the latter route offering the excuse that any tardy climbing is due to assiduously searching for water-borne debris! Not that anything is likely to be found. However, after a thirty minute or so climb, the impact area is attained by scaling the side of the gully to the left, shortly before it issues onto the rim. Yet here again, to reiterate, little is likely to be discovered, although contemporary photographs of the crash scene show what a job the aforementioned salvage party and Mr Shackleton faced. No debris is evident at the impact area – certainly not the carefully secreted fragment! – while the ageless hillside bears no scars. Nor, strangely, is there even a monument, here, or anywhere in the local area! For the walker, however, what a view! While the Hoarstone Edge gives access to what has to be one of the finest of rim paths.

From the gully's top, the crash site of PB4Y-1 Liberator 63934 (see above) is just 0.65 of a mile (1.05 km) distant on a heading of 209°M. The other relatively-nearby crash site is that of Tiger Moth T6464 (see below), easterly along the rim path, which is reached after one and a half miles, just before Chew Reservoir. If heading eastwards, however, a point to watch is that immediately after passing Rams Clough the rim path divides, the higher, right-hand branch being that which leads on along the ridge.

A safe return route from the Dakota site, regardless of the visibility, is that down either Rams Clough or the unnamed clough. Once fairly embarked upon the easterly rim path, however, then continuing to the Chew Reservoir and descending by Chew Road will probably serve best.

6. De Havilland DH82A Tiger Moth Mk.2 T6464
South-west of Chew Reservoir, Blindstones Moss

SE 03350 01592 505 m

Unit and Station: No. 24 Elementary Flying Training School,
RAF Sealand (Queensferry, near Chester),
No. 51 Group, Flying Training Command

Date: 12 April 1945

Crew: pilot: killed

- Sergeant Michael Augustine O'Connell, Royal New Zealand Air Force

De Havilland DH82A Tiger Moth

The de Havilland Tiger Moth, with a pedigree built upon the well-deserved reputation of the Moth tourer-cum-trainers which preceded it, went on to establish an even more illustrious reputation in its own right. Unashamedly a machine of the early 1930s and as unsophisticated as they come, it still proved a first-class trainer when used by Commonwealth-wide Elementary Service Flying Training Schools throughout the Second World War.

The Tiger Moth, although always docile, was never that easy to fly accurately. Besides which, although it was a sturdily-built machine, its instrumentation was little less than rudimentary. Therefore, with pupils being the valuable commodity they were, strict rules were laid down regarding flying in cloud. Indeed, RAF Sealand's relevant Unit Flying Order specified that they should not do so, but should, instead, expeditiously turn back on encountering either bad visibility or cloud. This was an order which every instructor and pupil pilot periodically signed as having 'read and understood'. Sergeant Michael O'Connell, of the Royal New Zealand Air Force, was among such signatories.

Tiger Moth cockpit

Sergeant O'Connell, stationed at RAF Sealand, near Chester, had completed one hour and forty minutes of a cross-country detail when he crashed and died near Chew Reservoir, forty-six miles from his base. The accident report does not specify whether Sergeant O'Connell was staff or pupil, but he had amassed a surprising number of flying hours for a pupil, 345 in total, with over 120 on Tiger Moths. He also claimed a considerable number of hours spent on instruments: 51 in the air, and 38 on the Link Trainer, the flight simulator of the day. Further, although he was a sergeant when the crash occurred, his promotion to flight sergeant had already been promulgated by the time his headstone was commissioned. No mystery there, though, for the ranks of Commonwealth casualties were habitually advanced in order to entitle relatives to the increased pension; for the RAF any such discrepancy was most often due to any promotion not having been promulgated at the time of death.

Setting aside any doubt regarding Sergeant O'Connell's status, his detail when he crashed was a solo day cross-country in the course of which he ran into a concentration of cloud. He did not turn back, however, but pressed on; only to become disorientated, to lose control, and to find himself unable to either recover or abandon before hitting the ground.

The court of inquiry did not mince matters. Unit Flying Orders laid down that pilots were not to continue flight in cloud; consequently the court found that Sergeant O'Connell had disobeyed orders by doing so, that he had then lost control when forced to rely solely upon his flight instruments – basic as they were – and crashed, destroying his machine and killing himself. Both the Air Officer Commanding and the Air Officer Commanding-in-Chief concurred with the finding, emphasizing thereby that even the Tiger Moth could, and would, bite if the safety rules were flouted.

In 2013 a fair pool of debris still remained, although it favoured concealing, rather than revealing, itself.

The debris pool in 2013. Chew Reservoir to the right. Immediately above the debris is the termination circle of the Chew Road: a not-too sedate, all-weather route for walkers

VISITING THE SITE

Having parked in the Dovestone Reservoir car park (see Section 4, above) a splendid way of visiting this site is to attain the Hoarstone Edge as detailed in Section five, then to follow the rim path south-easterly – keeping to the right where the path divides at Rams Clough! – towards Chew Reservoir, at the head of the Chew Valley. A more sedate, if still laborious-in-parts route, utilises the Chew Road, reaching Chew Reservoir after something like an hour and fifteen minutes.

Whether approaching along the rim path, or having ascended the Chew Road, some 280 yards after leaving the Reservoir and following the braided variant rim-path tracks, then at SE 03316 01670, the site lies 100 yards south-easterly (159°M) up the moor (at SE 03350 01592 505 m). Alternatively, from the Reservoir dam a discernible track seems to be in the making leading very nearly to the site. However, in all cases, the terrain is very broken, and the debris pool very small, so be prepared to search around from the coordinates given.

A safe return route for walkers, in any weather, is afforded by the Chew Road.

7. De Havilland DH98 Mosquito BMk.16 PF395
Chew Hills, above Dovestone Reservoir

SE 02570 03182 419 m, impact site

SE 02591 03179 408 m, debris pool

Unit and Station: No. 571 Squadron, RAF Oakington (north-west of Cambridge), No. 8 Group, Bomber Command

Date: 22 October 1944

Crew: two, both killed:

- Flying Officer Ernest Douglas Scotland, pilot
- Sergeant Humphrey Robert Cruse Soan, navigator

De Havilland Mosquito

The late-1941 de Havilland Mosquito, the 'all-wood' machine which its crews swore by, caught the public's fancy from the start. It impressed in all its many guises, but it was in its design role as a light bomber that it excelled. Its role, in fact, with No. 571 Squadron of Bomber Command, in October 1944 an element of the Fast Night-Striking Force, when Mosquito PF395 was one of the aircraft tasked to bomb a target in Hamburg.

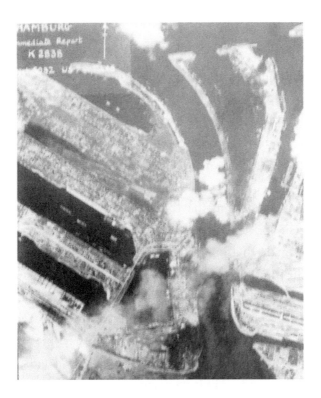

Target, Hamburg

The objective was successfully attacked, but on the way home to RAF Oakington the cockpit coolant gauge on PF395 showed a temperature rise which told its pilot, Flying Officer Ernest Scotland, that his port engine had suffered a glycol – engine-coolant – leak. Shortly afterwards he reported to others of the flight that he was shutting down the overheating engine.

Being deprived of an engine in a Mosquito, especially well on the way home from an operation, was no great matter. Indeed, many Mosquito groupies would hold that 'Sir' Geoffrey had designed the Mosquito as a single-engined aircraft and only added a second for the sake of appearance; as if in proof of which the prototype carried out a vertical climb with one engine stopped! Then again, although Flying Officer Scotland had only sixty hours on type he had some 1,600 hours' overall experience. For the crew of PF395, therefore, with reasonable weather and just the Cambridgeshire fenlands before them, there should have been no undue problem.

Losing half its power, of course, did mean that PF395 was no longer able to keep company with its fellows, who gradually forged ahead. Only, as they disappeared into the darkness – and one cannot imagine them doing so without the odd jocular remark to the laggard – so too did PF395's best hope vanish. For although the Mosquito was equipped with an engine-driven generator on both power plants, the last transmission received from Flying Officer Scotland was that all his onboard navigational equipment had now failed.

How chagrined he must have been, and how much more so his now blithely homebound fellow crews would later be, that the suggestion had not been made that one of them should throttle back and lag in his vicinity as a shepherdly guide! For had Flying Officer Scotland remained in company, then regardless of the state of his navigation and communication aids, by simply holding loose station he would have arrived, as all the others did, at their Cambridgeshire base. Except that his machine never did arrive.

Apart from the loss of their radio-navigational aids, what caused Flying Officer Scotland and his navigator, Sergeant Humphrey Soan, to go astray at that juncture was almost certainly the substantial sheet of cloud that had moved across the east of the country. For they not only overflew Oakington, but the whole of Cambridgeshire; in fact, they were next seen circling the eastern outskirts of Manchester, 120 miles to the north-west of Oakington, dipping below a ragged cloud base as they desperately sought to fix themselves. The word 'desperately' being used advisedly, because by the time of the sighting they had already been airborne an hour longer than the rest of the raiders, and fuel must have been running low.

The thought must have been in both their minds that, if they could not fix themselves very soon, the only option left to them would be to bale out; yet how reluctant any crew would be to follow that course; how pride would have militated against doing so, when all they needed was a single pinpoint!

Only as they searched, eyes intent without a doubt on the glow even then emanating from the blacked-out, yet still very evident, metropolis to the west, so their circling flight took them ever closer to the east, and to the high ground they had only just overflown. In fact, it could well be that they had finally succeeded in fixing themselves, and that they had already set course away from the area. Except that they flew into a rocky slope with 1,500 feet still indicating on their altimeter, Mosquito PF395 exploding around them, its sleek lines instantaneously fragmenting amid a life-snuffing welter of flames.

The debris pool beneath the impact point

The plateau debris pool, with the impact site diagonally above

The impact-area cache

Debris in the impact-area cache

VISITING THE SITE

Dovestone Reservoir from the impact site

Having parked in the Dovestone Reservoir car park (see Section 4), two routes offer themselves. The first is to ascend directly to the crash site from the bridge by the Life-for-a-Life commemorative woodland (ten minutes from the car park), climbing beside the gully which issues at SE 01976 03187, at 233 metres, the aiming level being that where grass gives way to rock. Reaching the crash site from the bridge requires a 700 foot climb and will take of the order of twenty minutes. Do not expect a proper path – popular though this upward route is at weekends –, but the slope, taken steadily, is kindly enough underfoot, with only occasional ankle-turning clumps of tussock grass: fortunately, that scourge seems to be reserving itself to swamp the now-meagre, stone-girdled fragments in the debris pool gathered on a plateau (at SE 02591 03179 408 m). This is reached by turning off-path to the left of the track just before the rock fringe begins its lift towards the summit ridge.

Daunting as the rocky fringe may appear, it proves to be easily within a walker's compass whether approaching from below, or from above: negotiated, of course, with all due care. The actual impact site is marked by a boulder cache of fragments lying 68 feet diagonally upwards (heading 099°M) from the debris pool, at SE 02570 03182, at 419 metres. Fragments are widespread between the two levels and soil slippages periodically reveal more.

The second route follows the Chew Road up to Chew Reservoir, then turns left to follow the Dish Stone Brow rim path, not shown on the map, but a fine track – if boggy near the reservoir – and indeed, beyond the crash site, arguably the most interesting of all the ridge routes in the area, what with its monuments and rock features, to say nothing of its grand views. This rim path runs along the 480 metre contour, the Mosquito impact site lying some 200 yards below the path (expect to take ten minutes or so in the descent).

To return to the car park when cloud has mantled the tops, reversing the direct route downhill is most to be favoured, taking of the order of twenty minutes to the bridges' area where it passes the prettiest of dell-like, picnic-worthy sites.

8. Westland Lysander Mk.3A V9403
Slate Pit Moss, north of Chew Reservoir

SE 04081 03254 520 m

Unit and Squadron: No. 6 Anti-Aircraft Co-operation Unit,
RAF Ringway (Manchester), No. 70 Group,
RAF Army Co-operation Command

Date: 19 August 1941

Crew: two, both injured, one mortally:

- Pilot Officer Frederick W. Hoddinott, pilot, injured
- Leading Aircraftman Alan Masheder Chadwick, wireless operator, died of his injuries

Pilot Officer Fred Hoddinott, 1941

Westland Lysander

The Westland Lysander was a rugged workhorse of a machine which, slow-flying, and, being capable of short landings and take-offs, became celebrated for its use in clandestine operations in occupied Europe. It had been designed, however, for the RAF's Army Co-operation Command whose tasks included exercising the personnel serving the guns, searchlights, sound-locators, listening posts, barrage-balloon sites and radar installations of the ground-defence organisation.

It was in furtherance of this main task that, in the early hours of 19 August 1941, Pilot Officer Frederick Hoddinott and his wireless operator, Leading Aircraftman Alan Chadwick, got airborne from Manchester's Ringway airfield. They were to fly a two-hour detail during which they were to liaise with the guns and searchlights covering the Rhyl sector. Air Defence considerations, however, did not permit Pilot Officer Hoddinott to fly directly to Rhyl, but initially obliged him to fly a south-westerly dog-leg around the Liverpool anti-aircraft balloon and gun defences which would take him all the way down to Chester before allowing him to turn for Rhyl.

His compass-setting procedure after take-off, on the other hand, would have been much more a matter of routine.

First, he would have turned his aircraft onto the pre-calculated heading for the initial leg using his magnetic compass. Next, he would have duplicated this heading on his complementary Directional-Gyro Indicator (DG), a gyroscopically stabilised heading indicator which, unlike the compass, did not hunt about in turbulence. Thereafter, with DG and compass matched, he would use the DG as his primary heading reference, resetting it against the compass periodically, and every time he settled onto any new leg.

It is a fundamental precept in aviation that the flier should always trust his instruments over his spatial instincts; but this is not to advocate a slavishly blind trust, for few aircraft instruments are as trustworthy as they might be, so that while directional aids harbour a multitude of inherent errors, other errors can only too easily be fed in by the user.

Any walkers will appreciate this, who, having set the required heading on their Silva-style compass, have then found themselves momentarily lining up the white end of the needle (instead of the red end) with the broad, red North arrow. They will know that, had they not realised what they had done, and failed, therefore, to turn themselves about, they would have been travelling in the opposite direction to that intended. Accordingly, because it was just as easy for a wartime aviator to do this, the mnemonic adopted was, 'Red on Red, full ahead': align the red needle with the red datum, and you were going in the correct direction. But inadvertently align the blue needle (of *their* compasses – white on the Silva) with the red datum, and you were off in the reverse direction: 'Red on Blue, this you'll rue'.

But compass errors aside it was also possible to mis-set the directional-gyro, either by not ensuring that its gyroscope was fully stabilised before making the adjustment, or by failing to set it to the correct heading: not a hard error to fall into given indifferent cockpit lighting.

An incidental way of checking on such gross errors was to get a directional bearing by wireless-telegraphy soon after take-off, which, although primarily aimed at proving the communications set, also proved the track being flown. In this instance, however, it seems probable that the machine's radio had been unserviceable from the outset.

As it was, Pilot Officer Hoddinott duly set off on his initial leg, finding himself in cloud in a very short time. Except that, some fifteen minutes along the leg, having made his first turn, he discovered a discrepancy between DG and compass of some one hundred and eighty degrees! Which meant that he might well have been flying on a reciprocal course, that is, heading north-easterly, instead of south-westerly.

This would have been a mind-numbing revelation, and one very difficult to readily assimilate, especially at night, in cloud, with a radio that was providing no assistance, and when flying at low level. For his altimeter was reading only 2,500 feet, and somewhere close by, out there in the cloud-filled night, the balloon-barrage defences – don't even think about the guns! – would be straining skywards on their cables, their sole purpose being to deter just such low-flying intruders as he had now become.

Hastily, Pilot Officer Hoddinott reassessed the situation, and (incorrectly) decided that his aircraft's directional-gyro must have been as faulty as its radio seemed to be. Reverting to his magnetic compass he turned south, and after a while, reasoning that he was now approaching the Cheshire Plain – an area, in general, less than three hundred feet above sea level – he began to descend in order to break clear of cloud. However, just as his altimeter was passing 1,900 feet so he flew into the ground. Both he and his wireless operator lost consciousness, eventually coming around to find themselves providentially alive, albeit injured to some degree, but helplessly trapped amidst the debris.

As dawn broke Pilot Officer Hoddinott realised that he was in a truly unenviable position. Instead of the lowland Cheshire Plain, he had clearly come down on some high-level moor. Further, if he had indeed flown the wrong way, then an aerial search of the area he actually found himself in was most unlikely. In the event, although he had crashed only seventeen miles north-east of Ringway, few search aircraft came that way. True, one circled tantalisingly over what Pilot Officer Hoddinott would later learn was the re-exposed remains of Swordfish P4223 which had crashed three miles to the east some eighteen months before (Part One, Section 15, see below). But although this search aircraft never suspected their presence its very concentration on the formerly buried debris further diverted the search effort. Indeed, the two men aboard the Lysander were to remain trapped throughout a second night before a Water Board worker at nearby Chew Reservoir happened to notice an unusual protuberance and set out across what, in 2013, was still a pathless and largely trackless moor, to investigate.

In the interim the situation of the survivors had been harrowing. With the initial shock of the crash receding, each had become conscious of his plight. For Pilot Officer Hoddinott, who could release only one leg from beneath the engine, thirst had outweighed his pain. But wireless operator Leading Aircraftman Alan Chadwick, with only debris in his field of vision, and with both legs painfully trapped, had quickly become despondent, his morale plummeting. Worse, however, was to befall him. For although his injuries had not been that serious in themselves, the sudden cessation of pressure when the wreckage was finally lifted from him left him open to the since well-documented 'crush syndrome', in which tissue damage and the release of toxins combine to produce a potentially fatal condition. In fact, although he was to linger for five more days, he was not to survive.

For Pilot Officer Hoddinott's part, his time on the moor had given him plenty of time to reflect upon what had gone wrong. Except that he had now (equally erroneously) settled the blame upon a faulty altimeter. He was well aware that a pressure altimeter, like a compass, suffers from inherent errors. As it was, it would take a map to persuade Pilot Officer Hoddinott that Slate Pit Moss – where he had crashed – was indeed at 1,700 feet above sea level. Despite which, when interviewed forty years later by author Ron Collier, he still persisted in believing that his instruments – whether compass, DG, or altimeter – had been faulty.

Pilot Officer Hoddinott's flight on a near-reciprocal heading has been likened, by some, to that of America's 'Wrong-way' Corrigan, who crossed the Atlantic in 1938 having ostensibly flown east when intending to fly west. The two cases were quite different, however, for Corrigan's 'error' had been the ploy he had adopted having been refused permission to make the eastward flight; the actual (red on blue) error being so commonplace that the outraged authorities, with public adulation against them, were able to save face and accept his claim. In reality, the Lysander epic had more in common with the British Hermes airliner which, in 1951, flew 900 miles astray over the Sahara and crashed, out of fuel, after its compass-system had been incorrectly set by a crew member.

In the Lysander's case the inquiry was to note that, although relatively experienced, having logged some one thousand hours' flying, Pilot Officer Hoddinott had flown only two hours at night on Lysanders, when familiarity with such 'switchery' as the setting of compasses and DGs was critical. It therefore found the cause to have been twofold. Firstly, that the aircraft had become airborne without the serviceability of its wireless being established; additionally noting that having no W/T would have significantly reduced its usefulness once at Rhyl. Secondly, and most significantly, that the aircraft had been flown on a reciprocal course.

Pilot Officer Hoddinott must have grieved a great deal during the many months of his convalescence, yet among the most poignant memories of the ordeal that he was to carry into his future flying would have been the plaintive reproach from his erstwhile crewman, the pain-racked voice coming forwards to him from the crumpled structure to his rear, 'But I thought you were a good pilot.'

In 2013 the crash site, although located on a particularly featureless stretch of moor, was marked by what must inevitably be merely evanescent traces of the Lysander. Just the same, a sprinkling of wooden splinters and some metal oddments had managed to survive, thinly splayed though they were across a patch of grass-starved peat.

The impact site, 2013

VISITING THE SITE

Parking in the Dovestone Reservoir car park is detailed in Section 4. After that it has to be said that this is a site which is rather further from a defined path than most in the area. Even so, the off-path excursion has certain attractions, and is not too onerous. The most convenient way to the heights, if not the most interesting, is to ascend the Chew Road to Chew Reservoir, some one and half miles (2.5 km) after the bridge beyond the Sailing Club at SE 01910 03161 – say an hour's upward plod. Once at the Chew Reservoir, its north-easterly-reaching wall, by chance, points directly to the crash site, 0.84 miles (1.4 km) distant. Beyond the wall, however, lies largely featureless moorland.

The Chew Dam wall

Then again (ignoring the wall pointer), there is a trail of sorts as far as the northern extension of the reservoir, and after that the gully of Small Clough gives a fair guide. Whichever of the two is taken, though, as off-path travel goes, this is as good as it gets, with coarse cotton-grasses rather than tussock grass underfoot and the often forlorn cries of meadow pippets, skylarks, Canadian Geese, and grouse, and even the occasional droop-snouted curlew, to keep company, any traverse of this particular moorland imparting a rather novel sense of isolation.

On reaching the Lysander site, the coordinates given are guaranteed, but what with the nature of the terrain, and depending upon the season's growth, what few fragments are left may still need searching for.

Regarding the return route, someone over five and a half foot tall may well be able to glimpse Chew Reservoir from the crash site, especially from one of the minor mounds near the site, but even in poor visibility the reservoir forms a backstop when reversing the outbound route.

Other walkers may choose to visit this site by climbing directly up the Chew Hill heights from the bridge beyond the sailing club (see Section 7), a far more interesting ascent to the rim than utilising Chew Road, and one favoured on a Sunday by a steady succession of family groups! Having reached the rim, the route for walkers visiting the Lysander site runs eastwards over the Dove Stone and Featherbed Mosses for some three-quarters of a mile (1.2 km); say thirty-five minutes. Again, there is that sense of isolation, but the moorland is not too rough, although the walker should not expect to actually see the north-south path the map has crossing their way! What is to be seen, and admired, particularly near the rim, are the numerous examples of formerly bare peat now so successfully resown with heather.

If choosing to return by reversing this cross-moorland route then – in good visibility, at least – the sense of isolation is somewhat lessened by a Manchester tower block serving to give the required line!

Mr Fred Hoddinott, 1982

Tintwistle Area

9. Hawker Hurricanes Mk.2C PZ851, PZ765, PZ854
Tintwistle Knarr, Longdendale Valley

SK 03569 98893 376 m

Unit and Squadron: No. 11 (Pilots) Advanced Flying Unit, RAF Calveley (north-west of Crewe), No. 21 Group, Flying Training Command

Date: 22 February 1945

Crew: pilots, three, all killed:

- Sergeant Ernest Mary Leon Marien, Belgian Air Force, leader (PZ851)
- Flight Sergeant Marcel Henry Leon Orban, Belgian Air Force (PZ765)
- Sergeant John Victor Robinson, RAF (PZ854)

Hawker Hurricanes in Vic formation

Thanks largely to the private-initiative drive of designer Sidney Camm and the Hawkers Aviation Company, the RAF was well served by its Hurricanes throughout the Second World War. The type was much modified but even the older marks gave sterling service to such training establishments as the Advanced Flying Unit at RAF Calveley which, on 22 February 1945, launched a trio of Hurricanes fated, lamentably, to add nothing to the aircraft's illustrious history.

The machines were flown by pupil pilots in the final stage of their flying training, each having something over 200 hours' flying in total and getting on for twenty on the Hurricane. The detail that day was to carry out a formation flight, with Sergeant Ernest Marien acting as the leader.

A section flying in line astern

It should be appreciated that, when flying in close formation, each pilot formating – holding station – on another will be concentrating solely on maintaining certain known alignments on that other pilot's machine; in line astern, for instance, on seeing rather more of the under surface of its wings, it might be, than of the upper surfaces, while at the same time keeping its tailplane at a given level on his own windshield. Conversely it is the formation leader's job to do the navigation; to look out for other aircraft; to ensure that fuel states and engine readings are regularly monitored; to see that gyroscopic instruments are re-stabilised against any inadvertent formation break-up which leaves individuals alone in cloud; in general, to *lead*, and above all to keep the formation clear of the ground.

After leaving RAF Calveley Sergeant Marien had headed in a generally north-eastwardly direction, exercising his section as he went. After some twenty minutes, though, having overflown Manchester, he called the trio into line astern and turned up the Longdendale Valley. There, however, although the weather was reasonable, the prevailing wind had brought in the city's industrial haze so that Sergeant Marien suddenly found himself flying in considerably reduced visibility. Wheeling around onto a northerly heading, almost certainly intending to clear from the valley, he became aware of ground rising steeply through the haze. Realising that he had inadvertently led his section towards a hillside he attempted to pull up and over; except that he was too low, and instead, he and his two hapless followers flew into the rocks at twelve hundred feet above sea level, well below the summit ridge, not bursting into flames, but with all three pilots dying instantly from the impact.

The inquiry's deliberations did not have to be lengthy: having taken his formation into conditions of poor visibility, at far too low a level, in a valley hedged about by high terrain, the leader had to bear the blame. Certainly none could devolve upon his numbers two and three, for their only responsibility had been to tuck in close and trust to their leader. But back at base their flight commander was duly disciplined – because two of the pilots involved had failed to sign the flying order book before departure!

A threefold tragedy. But how especially grievous that two of those trainee pilots had gone to such lengths to join up with the RAF and carry on the fight, escaping from German-Occupied Belgium with all the hazards that entailed. So what a tragedy in itself, that all those high patriotic hopes should be so futilely dashed upon an English upland!

Mr Bob Sie, of Doveholes, remembered the scene the day after the crash, when he was accompanying his father, a quarryman lorry driver. 'The wreckage was widespread on the slope,' he said, 'but well guarded by RAF men who were burning some bits, and preparing to bring other stuff down.' In similar vein Mr George Sherratt, formerly of Whitfield Barn Farm, Glossop, recalled, 'The day after the crash my friend, Ken Bancroft, who used to visit all the local crashes, went up there to see what was what and to get some souvenirs, only to be turned away by the police. But for ages there were what looked like three shell holes in the hillside, one above the other.'

Mr Wright Cooper

The most intimately involved witness, however, was Mr Wright Cooper, of Townhead Farm, Tintwistle. 'It was a very misty day,' he recalled, 'and I was working on the slopes, spreading manure, when suddenly these three Hurricanes appeared. They came from the Broadbottom direction, and they were so low I thought they were going to take my head off. They didn't seem to be in formation, one was high, while the lowest one actually went under the power lines – at that time there were big pylons on the Tintwistle side of the valley, though they've been repositioned on the far side since. I knew full well what they were heading into, so I mouthed, "You've had it." And just an instant later I heard this triple thump through the mist.' He paused. 'I rushed up there, and found that the pilot of the lowest one was still in his seat; but clearly dead. The one immediately above him had struck in much the same way, nose first. But the highest one must have seen the hill, for he'd pulled up and was pretty well flat on the slope.' He paused again. 'I can't describe how gruesome it was. But strangely, what struck me even then, was that although the propellers were smashed, together with virtually everything else, the engines were complete, and I remember thinking how well made they must have been. There was no fire – for what it was worth.'

Seeing the three Hurricanes coming at him head on, Mr Cooper's impression had been that they were not formating; that is, not flying in the so-familiar 'Vic'. In fact, what he found was clearly a trio in 'section line astern' formation. This meant that Sergeant Marien's number two would have been sitting directly behind, and just below, Sergeant Marien's tail; that his number three would have been holding a similar station on the number two: the number two then, must have passed above the power lines by as narrow a margin as the 'lowest one', the number three, had passed below them! The two followers, accordingly, totally intent on holding station, would never have seen the hillside looming up. Sergeant Marien, on the other hand, was afforded just sufficient time to haul back on the stick. But not an instant more …

'If onlys' are always pointless, and arguably never more so than in air-accident investigation, yet eyeing the terrain, the inescapable fact is that had only the leader been heading two or three degrees further left, the trio would have missed the rising slope and passed over lower ground, leaving ample room to climb above the higher ground further on, never to know how they had been hazarded. As it was, the two followers, at least, died without such harrowing awareness.

Regarding the crash site, it would seem that those airmen subsequently seen clearing it did a good job, and that the passage of time, and more-persistent souvenir collectors, pretty well finished off the task, for there was little enough left of the three aircraft in 2013, merely a few grey scraps of metal enclosed within a circlet of rocks amid a steeply sloping hillside full of tumbled boulders, heather, and dark-hued scree.

Debris from all three aircraft in a single pool, 2013

VISITING THE SITE

The most convenient parking is off the very busy A628 Woodhead Road (between Crowden and Tintwistle) at SK 03964 98323 200 metres, but this has room for only four or so properly parked vehicles (alternative parking exists at SK 03436 97934, a half mile further west along the trunk road). A well made zig-zag track then leads conveniently upwards while a steeper, more direct trail follows the boundary of the woods. After some ten minutes, and above the zig-zag, the trail passes a wooden memorial cross at SK 03637 98649, at 308 metres, which bears a plaque commemorating those killed in the three nearest crashes. The trail then carries on up and over the first hillside-shoulder, passing closest to the Hurricanes' crash site at SK 03502 98888, at 375 metres. The debris pool then lies just seventy yards off to the east, but being located amid rocks, heather, and somewhat stunted trees, and being so small, it might well need searching for.

The quickest way back to the parking spot is to reverse the outbound route. Having visited the site, however, it is more than likely that the walker will wish to carry on to the nearby sites of P-38 Lightning 42-67270 and Lancaster PA411, in which case it is still best to return to the trail, then continue upwards on the path. The alternative, forging directly upwards from the site itself, through rock-concealing thigh deep heather, is markedly unproductive!

Introducing an unashamed, teaching-grandmother, cautionary note: having safely accomplished the foray and returned to the car, take great care in exiting onto the A628, for even the tiniest juggernauts rush past at a mind-numbing rate!

Looking ahead along the line of flight

10. Lockheed P-38J Lightning 42-67207
Tintwistle Knarr, Longdendale Valley

SK 03932 99080 444 m

Unit and Squadron: United States Eighth Army Air Force,
8th Air Force Composite Command,
496th Fighter Training Group, 554th Fighter Training Squadron,
AAF345 (RAF Goxhill), 12 miles north-west of Grimsby

Date: 10 May 1944

Crew: pilot, killed

• Flight Officer Hugh Allen Jones, United States Army Air Force

Lockheed P-38 Lightning

By 1944 the twin-engined, twin-boomed P-38 Lightnings were making their mark as long-range escorts for the American daylight bombers penetrating deep into enemy territory. This was not without cost, of course, so a constant stream of replacements for both machines and pilots was required to keep the operational squadrons up to strength, the job of initiating such new pilots into European-theatre conditions falling to fighter-training groups like the Goxhill-based 496th.

On 10 May 1944 Flight Officer Hugh Jones was detailed as one of a section of P-38 pilots who were to carry out a sequence of exercises. These were to include cine-gun practice in engagements with other P-38s; then formation flying, single-engined operation, and navigation on instruments at a specified 'over 5,000 feet' altitude; an intriguing mixture for any leader to tie into a coherent sequence. However, on getting airborne, Flight Officer Jones failed to join up with his own section, and instead, joined a pair who had been briefed to carry out a similar mixed-bag sortie.

The leader of this pair, accepting the stray lamb which had appeared on his right wing, headed west from Grimsby, and was to hold that general heading for twenty minutes while exercising his extempore trio in various instrument manoeuvres, his eventual intention being, as he later testified, to 'pin-point on Manchester'. As he neared the zone of high ground, however, he encountered thick cloud, and having descended to 2,500 feet in an attempt to find space beneath it, discovered that it extended to ground level. He then initiated a left-hand half-circle in order to bring his three aircraft into clear air once more; except that, on emerging from cloud just thirty seconds later, it was to discover that Flight Officer Jones had failed to keep station, and was missing.

Later, the American authorities were advised that Flight Officer Jones's machine had crashed and burnt out on the shoulder of Tintwistle Knarr, above Longdendale's Valehouse Reservoir. Examination of the site then revealed that the P-38 had crashed inverted and at a shallow angle, from which the accident investigators concluded that Flight Officer Jones, no longer able to keep station, and so being forced to an instant reliance on his flight instruments in cloud, had lost control.

Loss of control could also have occurred if, on transferring his attention from his leader's machine into his own cockpit, Flight Officer Jones had found his gyroscopically-stabilised flight-attitude instruments toppled – the result of a few minutes of tension-breaking follow-my-leader aerobatic chasing, perhaps? But this would have been no cause for concern had he only managed to maintain station in that final turn, for then he would have had no call upon his own instruments.

The state of his flight-instrument gyros aside, however, being relatively inexperienced, and beyond that, trained for the most part as a 'clear-sky' day-fighter pilot, it is probable that he simply found himself unable to cope with the demands of a shock transition onto instrument flight.

But there was another factor. For, having once lost control when the formation turned at the leader's declared 2,500 feet on the altimeter, and over ground elevated to 1,640 feet above sea level, the 900 feet of sky Flight Officer Jones had been left with was precious little for him to either regain control or bale out; even had he broken cloud before impact.

Unsurprisingly the accident was attributed to '100% pilot error, with Error of Technique underlain by Inexperience'. Inexplicably, however, the compilers of the statistical section of the accident report, while recording Flight Officer's Jones's 300 hours' total flying, not only omitted his recent instrument-flying history, but positively dismissed instrument flying as being 'Not a factor'. And inexplicably? Because the final recommendation was 'That more instrument flying, and more cloud flying technique, be taught in the Operational Training Unit Course'!

Mr Wright Cooper

Farmer Wright Cooper, of Tintwistle, spoke sombrely of that day. 'I was shepherding on Robinson's Moss,' he recalled, 'when this plane dived almost vertically into the ground. I was only a few hundred yards away, so I rushed across, but found that there was nothing to be done. The pilot's torso had been flung clear. And everything else was in pieces too. Some Water Board men had been working on the lower slopes and they soon joined me. Then one of them went down to the Bottoms Reservoir office, and had the alarm raised.'

As Mr Cooper had found on reaching the scene, and as the American investigating officer later recorded, when the aircraft impacted and exploded, its wreckage was spread across an area '100 yards long and fifty wide'.

Regarding the recovery, 'The Americans,' Mr Cooper explained, 'winched most of the big stuff down. They'd wind in the cable as far as they could, then re-position their winch lower down, until eventually they reached their vehicles. Just the same, a lot of bits were left.' By 2013, however, the leavings had dwindled to a moderate pool of debris.

The debris pool in 2013

VISITING THE SITE

The most popular route is that described for visiting the Hurricanes' site (see above). Continuing upwards from SK 03502 98888, at 375 metres, the trail intersects with an east-west path which may not be quite as obvious on the ground as on the map. However, if that is missed, then any eastwards-leading patch relatively clear of heather and bilberry will prove useful during the 500-yard trek. Also, some faint 'visitor' trails do become apparent near the crash site. Just the same, despite the proven coordinates, it may be necessary to cast about in order to locate the debris pool, for although there was still a substantial of wreckage in 2013 it was standing in a veritable sea of rock-strewn heather. A visual guide, given fair weather, may be taken from the woods and the farm across the valley shown on the accompanying photograph.

To return to the car, the most convenient way is to backtrack. Yet many crash-site visitors might well consider continuing from this location to that of Lancaster PA411 just 440 yards away on a heading of 298°M. The off-path going is easier this close to the summit but although unavoidable patches of heather might make life difficult during the transit they will not make progress too difficult.

11. Avro Lancaster BMk.1 PA411
Tintwistle Knarr, north-east of Glossop

SK 03570 99254 438 m

Unit and Station: No. 230 Operational Conversion Unit (OCU),
RAF Lindholme (near Doncaster), No. 1 Group, Bomber Command

Date : 21 December 1948

Crew: seven, all killed:

- Flight Lieutenant Thomas Iowerth Johnson, pilot, OCU instructor
- Flight Sergeant Jack Sherwood Thompson, pilot
- Flight Lieutenant Peter Maskell, navigator
- Flight Sergeant Robert Smith, air signaller, OCU instructor
- Sergeant William Love, air signaller
- Flight Sergeant David Harris, flight-engineer, OCU instructor
- Flight Sergeant Vincent Graham, flight-engineer

Lancaster PA411

The function of the Operational Conversion Unit (The Operational *Training* Unit throughout the Second World War) was to bring together members of the respective aircrew categories and teach them to operate the machines they would fly on first-line squadrons. Some crew members might only just have gained their wings, or brevets, others might be experienced aircrew changing types or even roles. So on 20 December 1948, when OCU staff pilot Flight Lieutenant Thomas Johnson got airborne on a night-familiarisation training sortie, three of his pupil crew were being 'screened' in their respective specialisations by instructors overlooking their operation.

A typical pattern for such a sortie would have been to clear the circuit and climb away into uncluttered airspace. Once away from the airfield the trainee crew could then begin to assimilate any differences between day and night handling; not least getting used to the switches and dials as illuminated by the aircraft's lighting alone, and almost certainly learning to deal with engine failures by stopping various engines in order to familiarise all aboard with the problems posed by asymmetric flight at night.

Having sufficiently exercised each crew member in his own province, Flight Lieutenant Johnson would then have directed a return to the airfield to join the circuit and allow the trainee pilot to get to grips with night-time landings and take-offs. Since getting airborne, however, Lancaster PA411 had been perambulating around the sky as the wind and the various manoeuvres took it, the pilots concentrating on the handling and leaving the navigator to keep track of where they actually were. Except that at some stage during the homing a 'very strong radio signal' (according to the accident report) convinced the flying pilot that he was actually overhead Lindholme. At which – with the navigator offering nothing contradictory – he commenced his descent.

Unappreciated by any on board, however, as they were now over thick cloud, and owing to the combination of the arbitrary patterns flown and an insidious drifting with the wind, they were a full forty miles to the west of Lindholme and not that many feet above the Peak District highlands. So it was that their confident descent through cloud was abruptly terminated by the obdurate presence of Tintwistle Knarr, the aircraft bursting into flames on impact, disintegrating, and throwing clear some members of the crew, none of whom survived for any length of time.

Lancaster PA411 on Tintwistle Knarr, photo by courtesy of Mrs Margaret Buxton-Doyle, vice her father, Mr Harry Buxton, **Glossop Chronicle**

The detached tailplane, with Mr Max Webberley, editor of the **Glossop Chronicle,** *courtesy of Mrs Margaret Buxton-Doyle*

First on the scene were five members of the Bagshaw family of Old Road, Tintwistle, who had witnessed the explosion. Mr John Bagshaw told the *Glossop Chronicle* how he and his four sons (Jack, Basil, Neville, and Ernest) had accomplished a thirty-minute climb to the site, 'with no moon, and … no lantern', but guided by the fires. The newspaper account described in harrowing detail what the Bagshaws had found there; suffice to say here that it was evident to them that nothing could have been done for any of the crew.

Thanks to prompt alerting, the rescue services arrived at the scene in good time, after which the laborious undertaking of bringing the bodies down to the Hollingworth mortuary got under way.

This loss, tragic though it was in human terms, would have been a double blow to the unit, for the captain of the aircraft, Flight Lieutenant Johnson, although not at the controls at the time of the crash, but overseeing his pupil, was a pilot whose level of experience had risen to some 1,700 hours; a level which should have equipped him with command skills enough to keep him attentive to the wider picture. Notwithstanding that in all instruction, and in flying instruction in particular, there is a fine line to be observed between stultifying the development of the student – and prospective captain, in this case – by over-monitoring, and the alternative of standing too far back.

So it was that the court of inquiry had to lodge charges of poor airmanship against Flight Lieutenant Johnson; firstly, for not double-checking on the navigator's performance, and secondly, for allowing the trainee pilot to descend through cloud without having definitely established their position himself. The only positive recommendation that could be made, retrospective perforce, was that, in the future, navigators on the unit must determine their position at fifteen-minute intervals whenever engaged in such free-ranging exercises.

Mr Wright Cooper, of Tintwistle's Townhead Farm, immediately below the Knarr, did not actually visit this crash site at the time, and who would wonder after his gruesome discoveries as first arrival at both the nearby P-38 and triple-Hurricane crashes. 'I was out snaring rabbits on another part of the moor,' he explained, 'but when I saw all the lights I guessed what must have happened. Only, even from that distance I could see other people there. So it was clear that whatever could be done, had been.' Researcher Mr Arnold Willerton, of Hyde, for his part, harboured a poignant memory of the aftermath of the tragedy. 'The day afterwards,' he remembered, 'as we left Mottram by bus, we could see the debris sparkling all across the face of Tintwistle Knarr.'

Over the years, however, and despite the remote location of the crash site, high above the Rhodeswood Reservoir, most of the wreckage has disappeared, much disposed of by an enterprising local scrap dealer, utilising, in part, it is held, a Reliant Robin three-wheeler as transport! Certainly in 2013 little remained but a few heavy components high in a stony gully on the south-western flank of brooding Tintwistle Knarr.

The site on Tintwistle Knarr in 2013

VISITING THE SITE

The most direct route to the Lancaster site follows that described for viewing the Hurricanes (see above). Continuing upslope from the position used as a stepping-off point for this (SK 03502 98888, 375 m), the Lancaster's debris is 420 yards distant on a heading of 010°M. Two substantial footpaths, east-west in this vicinity, will be crossed, of which the second, soon to wend northwards, might be utilised for quite some way. This detour may prove unnecessary, however, for although the heather and bilberry still conceals rocks, this near-summit region is far more open and the going, overall, not too bad. Before 2012 the rock-strewn slope into which the Lancaster impacted was actually clear of heather, but regeneration programmes are widespread and there were marked changes by 2013. Walkers wishing to return to the parking area can most usefully reverse the outbound routing. It could, be however, that the intention would be to take in the crash site of Chipmunk WB579 on Arnside Moor, 0.64 miles (1.3 km) distant on a heading of 310°M. To save unnecessary labour, however, before setting out best refer to the walker's guide to that site (see below).

12. De Havilland Chipmunk TMk.10 WB579
Arnfield Moor, Tintwistle

SK 02738 99870 407 m

Unit and Squadron: No. 2 Reserve Flying School,
RAF Flying Training Command, Barton (west of Manchester)

Date: 3 July 1951

Crew: pilot, unhurt

- Pilot Officer Harry Bate Wright, RAF Volunteer Reserve

De Havilland Chipmunk

The Chipmunk was the worthy replacement for the redoubtable Tiger Moth biplane trainer and became the mainstay of the RAF's Volunteer Reserve units. However, although easy to fly in a general way it was a very demanding machine to operate with precision. Always lurking too was a spin characteristic which could – and on occasion did – bite, retrospective anti-spin modifications notwithstanding. But such characteristics aside, it was among the most pleasant of aircraft to fly, as Pilot Officer Harry Wright of the Volunteer Reserve was well aware when he got airborne from Barton, near Manchester, on 3 July 1951.

With an authorisation that included low flying he set off intent on carrying out a local-area detail to the east of Barton, only to find that, having overflown a layer of cloud, he could discover no breaks. At which stage, suddenly uncertain of his position, but believing himself to be far nearer the airfield than he actually was, he carried out a blind let-down, emerging into rain. The rain drastically reduced the below-cloud visibility, so that, even as he looked into the cockpit to refer to his compass, he flew into rising moorland, the fixed undercarriage somersaulting the Chipmunk onto its back to leave Pilot Officer Wright dangling upside down in his straps.

The wrecked Chipmunk, photo by courtesy of Mrs Margaret Buxton-Doyle, vice her father, Mr Harry Buxton, **Glossop Chronicle**

Although uninjured, Pilot Officer Wright experienced some difficulty in safely extricating himself from his inverted cockpit; pilots had been known to break their necks escaping from such a predicament! Having won clear, however, he then made his way down the moor to what he was to discover was Arnfield Farm, a mile and a half from the wreck of his aircraft, and fifteen miles east of his Barton base. The incumbent, tenant farmer Mr John Highley, told the *Glossop Chronicle* that Pilot Officer Wright had said it had seemed like hours before he had been able to dig his way out of the peat blocking the cockpit, while a Mrs Thompson ('one of the residents', as the paper had it) made the point that the shocked pilot had been so mired with peat that it had been hard to tell that he was in uniform. Once the wreck was discovered, as the *Chronicle* faithfully recorded, it was dealt with by airmen from the RAF Maintenance Unit at Bowlee, Manchester.

The board of inquiry – by 1951 'court' of inquiry had given place to 'board' – found that Pilot Officer Wright had entered cloud rather than turning back on encountering it, as his Unit Flying Orders required. Additionally it found that he had let down blind rather than climbing up until he had altitude enough to ensure that he could obtain a radio homing to base. He was also called to account for not taking sufficient note of compass-turning errors, or alternatively for lack of care in setting his directional indicator against his compass; the argument being that having adopted the correct procedure for either would have freed his eyes from the cockpit at the critical time.

Speaking of the incident, Mr Wright Cooper, of the neighbouring Townhead Farm, picked up on the fact that the hapless pilot had escaped injury despite his machine being inverted. 'Johnny Highley, my lifelong friend,' he said heavily, 'who took him in, didn't have the same luck some years later when his tractor tipped over on him …' And Mrs Thompson? One of the residents? Mr Cooper brightened. 'That was Katey, Johnny's girl friend, though the papers didn't like to say so at the time.' He paused, and then added warmly, 'She was flighty –, but Oh! what a *bonny* girl.'

On the afternoon of the crash, mist and drizzle had prevented the salvage party from locating the wreckage, but the next day, with clear weather, the aircraft had been sighted without difficulty. A circumstance which, it might be felt, had set a pattern, for although in 2013 a small pool of wreckage still remained to mark the impact site, yet with the ground being so broken and with heather abounding, there have been some good-weather searchers – certainly this one, back in 2005 – who, having approached from Tintwistle Knarr and the shooting cabins, actually reached the reference given, yet went away frustrated; only to see the site from half-a-mile off next time, on approaching from Arnfield.

The Arnfield site, 2013

In 2013 former Pilot Officer Wright wrote: I was the pilot – still kicking and enjoying retirement in Melbourne, Australia. Takes me back to the bloody hands after escaping the broken cockpit, and the lady farmer at Arnfield farm on answering the door to find a rather muddied figure unable to speak – I then realised what shock was! After taking in the situation she took me inside for a cuppa, and after recovering and explaining said 'Well, you are one lucky son of a gun'. Have since enjoyed much flying in Sailplanes - beautifully serene and no petrol to worry about!

VISITING THE SITE

The most comfortable way to visit this site is to start at Tintwistle and (from SK 02194 97329) drive up Arnfield Lane until convenient – and considerately chosen – parking can be found in the vicinity of Arnfield Farm (at SK 01589 98056 208 m). A shooters' track then leads to the north-east for a mile and a quarter to reach two shooting cabins (at SK 03020 99416 375 metres). After this a similar track continues (now on 015°M) for about 350 yards to SK 03124 99726 413 metres. Beyond this there is no path, the remaining 440 yards involving holding the height on a heading of 295°M while searching out stretches of low heather and negotiating the not-that-onerous Arnfield Gutter. The return simply reverses this route.

An alternative approach is to park by the A628 (between Crowden and Tintwistle, at SK 03964 98323 200 m) and approach the Chipmunk site from that of Lancaster PA411 on Tintwistle Knarr (see above). It is perfectly possible to take a straight-line course from one to the other, heading 310°M for 0.64 miles (1 km) and taking Arnfield Clough in one's stride. This, though, can be a daunting slog, for despite the attractiveness of the embryo Arnfield Brook, its steep slopes are thick with unremitting boulder-laced heather.

In truth, if approaching from the Lancaster site, it is much easier to embark upon a mile-long walk around the head of Arnfield Clough, maintaining the contour (of 440 metres or so) and crossing the stream at SK 03755 99877. After that, still holding the height until Arnfield Gutter is crossed at SE (Confirmed, *SE!*) 03067 00029, leaves just 400 yards of descent, on 238°M, to the Chipmunk crash site at SK (back to *SK!*) 02738 99870, at 407 metres.

In early 2013 a small pool of wreckage remained but although the coordinates supplied are dependable, and regardless of the approach utilised, seeing the pool might require a good lookabout. A convenient line-up point, in good visibility, is the gap in the woods towards Arnfield shown in the accompanying photo.

The return route to reach Arnfield reverses that used outbound, rejoining the now south-westerly Arnfield track at the shooting cabins. Conversely, returning to a car parked by the A628 can least laboriously be done by taking a south-of-easterly heading from the cabins then crossing Arnfield Clough on the most convenient-seeming line for the (dried-up) reservoir at SK 03259 98906, at 349 metres (an industrial relic well worth while pausing by). After that, the way leads off-path through the least obstructive heathery patches to the brick-built mini-reservoir at SK 03573 98676 to pick up the trail descending beside the Didsbury Intake Woods to the zig-track and so, to the parking area.

Again, an unashamed homily-finger wag, the excursion complete, the greatest care should be taken in nosing out of the lay-by onto the lorry-laden A628.

Black Hill Area

13. Consolidated-Vultee B-24H-20 Liberator 42-94841
Twizle Head Moss, Lightens Edge, Holme Moss

SE 10684 03573 493 m, impact point

SE 10670 03449 498 m, port gear

SE 10629 03383 505 m, terminal site

Unit and Squadron: United States Eighth Army Air Force, 492nd Bombardment Group, 857th Bombardment Squadron, AAF 179 (RAF Harrington), west of Kettering, Northants

Date: 9 October 1944

Occupants: ten, two passengers and seven crew killed, one crew member survived:

- First Lieutenant Elmer D. Pitsenbarger, pilot
- Second Lieutenant James D. Nendal, co-pilot
- Flight Officer Jack M. Bliss, navigator
- Flight Officer Frank Cser, bombardier (survived impact for some hours)
- Technical Sergeant Presley E. Farris, engineer
- Technical Sergeant Joseph W. Zwinge, radio operator
- Staff Sergeant Curtiss Anderson, waist gunner (survived, critical injuries)
- Staff Sergeant Frank A. Villelli, tail gunner
- Corporal Clarence S. Watson, passenger, non-aircrew rated
- Corporal Charles T. Lowblad, passenger, non-aircrew rated

Consolidated-Vultee B-24H-20 Liberator

The Consolidated Vultee B-24 Liberator bomber had a healthy cruising speed exceeding 220 mph (190 knots) at low level but its rate of climb of only a thousand feet a minute meant that the determination of a safe height to fly was of particular importance. As was only too starkly demonstrated on 9 October 1944 when B-24 42-94841 was flown into Twizle Head Moss, above the village of Holme, near Holmfirth.

Having arrived in England in early June 1944, just prior to the D-Day landings in occupied France, First Lieutenant Elmer Pitsenbarger's crew had been engaged in bombing raids over Germany, and later, in transport-support missions into France. On 9 October, following an acclimatisation course designed to further familiarise him with flying in temperate conditions over hilly terrain, First Lieutenant Pitsenbarger was detailed to air test a repaired aircraft which another crew was to fly on an operational mission later that day. The proving test was to be carried out as an integral part of a navigational exercise that was to route via Goole, Huddersfield, Stafford, Builth Wells, Worcester, Banbury, and so back to Harrington, the specific weather briefing being to remain in sight of the ground throughout. At 1415 hours, therefore, carrying just eight of his normal ten-man crew, but with two, joy-riding, non-aircrew passengers aboard, First Lieutenant Pitsenbarger took off in the aircraft its regular crew had christened 'Sack Time'.

The first two legs were completed without undue incident, but then came the south-westerly leg from Huddersfield to Stafford. Another pilot, whose aircraft had preceded First Lieutenant Pitsenbarger's on the route by twenty minutes, later reported that low stratus was actually hanging on the high ground throughout this leg. Yet although the topographical map shows several spot heights of nearly two thousand feet bracketing the track, 'Sack Time' was seen heading towards the cloud-shrouded 1,728-feet-above-sea-level Holme Moss at such a low altitude as to alarm those it overflew. An alarm well justified, for shortly after the machine disappeared into the cloud there was a dull thud as it impacted into the high ground.

The aircraft had, in fact, been within a mile of its intended track when it struck the ground just above the rim of 1,600-feet-above-sea-level

Lightens Edge. On impact it had gouged a wide groove through the peat and careered on for some two hundred yards, shedding pieces as it went before bursting into flames.

It seems probable that both the co-pilot and the engineer, the latter positioned behind the captain's seat, actually saw the ground an instant before impact, for their arms were found to be lifted, as if to ward off the danger; the majority of the others, who would have been enjoying the low-level views, and were therefore not strapped in, were killed instantly. Two men, however, survived to be taken off the moor. Flight Officer Frank Cser, the bombardier, was carried down to a hospital, only to die in the early hours of the next morning. Staff Sergeant Curtiss Anderson, however – 'I'm from California', he greeted rescuers –, although suffering injuries that would involve him in surgery until late 1946, eventually made a reasonable recovery.

Rescuers were soon on the scene, but once they left the road they found actually crossing the moorland to be an arduous undertaking. Nor was their task made any easier as they neared the burning bomber by exploding bullets zipping about their ears. Mr Kenneth Denton, of Holme, who as a youth of fifteen took his turn in helping with Staff Sergeant Anderson's stretcher, vividly remembered the sharp detonations punctuating the crackling of the engulfing flames. 'But I was too intent on the task in hand', he said, 'to be over-concerned.'

It was to prove a busy night for all those involved in the rescue effort, whether Police, Fire Service, Ambulance, or civilian volunteer helper, like Mr Denton; and even then the task was to be extended, because, when it was established that one of the passengers was still unaccounted for, a series of searches was mounted into the surrounding moors; searches which were only called off days later when a heavy section of wreckage was lifted for removal, to reveal the body of Corporal Clarence Watson underneath.

The Accident Investigation Committee had little to do, for they had the evidence of the pilot of the preceding aircraft regarding the cloud disposition, and witnesses who had seen First Lieutenant Pitsenbarger's aircraft flying at a fatally low altitude. In their summary, therefore, they were unequivocal in attributing the accident to 80% pilot error, finding that Lieutenant Pitsenbarger had shown poor judgement in not returning to base when such bad weather was encountered 'as this was not an operational flight'.

Walkers – Mr Ian Pell and Mr Melvyn Stephenson – at the main terminal site, 2011

A secondary site

In 2013 the crash site retained a distinctive scar where the machine struck Lightens Edge. Then came a two-hundred-and-twenty-yard stretch over which debris was strewn, including minor and major locations where the main section of the Liberator had burnt out, the two patches being yet devoid of vegetation.

The impact site, looking along the line of flight

Looking back from the impact site towards Holmfirth, 2013

VISITING THE SITE

Adequate parking is available at the Holme Moss Summit car park (SE 09808 03901 500 m) to the east of the A6024 Woodhead Road, with additional, more limited space higher up beside the television mast, at SE 09615 03687, 523 metres.

Heading north-east from the main car park for some 160 yards, a convenient footpath – with spectacular views towards Holmfirth and the *Last of the Summer Wine* country – can be picked up at SE 09929 03966 500 m, some 200 feet above that marked on the map. This then runs above the boundary wall of Lightens Edge for 900 yards to the south-east before reaching a gully at SE 10708 03700, 467 metres.

Turning southerly up this gully leads, after 150 yards of grough-cut heather, to the initial impact point (at SE 10684 03573 500 m), then (in 2013) to an undercarriage leg 126 yards further on, and finally to the terminal point, 90 yards beyond; in all, a 35 minute walk from the car park. It is noteworthy that in recent years the debris which was formerly on the actual impact-point scar (coordinates as given) has been moved some yards further on and pooled by another area equally bare of heather in early 2013, although regeneration is widespread across the whole moor.

It is, of course, perfectly possible to leave the car park and walk off-path directly to the site, following in the footsteps of the rescue party. This is not too onerous, especially at the beginning of a day's foraying, requiring a grough-and-heather bash of 0.57 miles (0.9 km) on a heading of 114°M to reach the initial impact scar, or 0.6 miles (say 1 km) on a heading of 127°M for the terminal site. To return to the car park in poor visibility, the Woodhead Road forms a safe backstop, with reversing the outbound route above the Lightens Edge boundary wall as a somewhat less strenuous alternative.

14. North American Sabre Mk.2 19234
Holme Moss, near Holme, and Holmfirth

SE 09133 05087 533 m, impact point
SE 09106 05071 533 m, main site
SE 09059 05030 533 m, tertiary site
Unit and Squadron: Royal Canadian Air Force,
No. 137(T) Flight, Ringway (Manchester)
Date: 14 December 1954
Crew: pilot: killed

- Flying Officer Patrick V. Robinson, Royal Canadian Air Force

North American Sabre

In 1954 the Royal Canadian Air Force was occupying RAF stations in Britain as part of its 'Cold War' commitment. On 14 December 1954 one of its Sabres, part of a batch to be made over to the Greek Air Force, had been undergoing servicing at the maintenance depot at Ringway, Manchester. Emerging from the hangar towards evening, now sporting its Greek colours, it was to be test-flown by Flying Officer Patrick Robinson. Some time after take-off, however, and in conditions of poor visibility, the machine was seen to pass relatively low over Holme in the direction of the 1,700-feet-above-sea-level Holme Moss. Then, shortly after it had passed into the gloom, the concerned watchers, seeing a brief glow high in the mist followed by the sound of an impact, knew only too well what had happened.

Rescue efforts were soon under way but the weather made the crash difficult to find; and even when the site was eventually located it became clear that the task was one of salvage rather than rescue. For the Sabre had flown directly into the moor and skidded on, shedding wings and other components as it went. It had also torn Flying Officer Robinson from his ejection-seat harness, thrown him through the canopy, and tumbled him a full eighty yards further on along the line of flight.

The inquiry had little to do in finding that the aircraft had simply been flown too low, Flying Officer Robinson having taken no account of the terrain.

In recent years re-seeding the site of the initial impact point has resulted in its debris being moved closer to the main debris site, the 2013 disposition being detailed below.

VISITING THE SITE

Holme Moss summit, on the A6024 Woodhead Road, offers generous parking, the higher, smaller area (at SE 09615 03687 523 m) coinciding with the pathway that runs, vestigially for the most part – indeed, in early 2013 crying out for paving! –, to the west of the television mast. This then parallels Heydon Brook to reach Heydon Head (at SE 08448 04733 561 m) after just under a mile (1.6 km), a thirty-minute walk. From this point, where the path turns away and crosses the brook, there is only rough walking, the main Sabre debris lying 800 yards off on a heading of 058°M. For many years now passage over the intervening, and very broken ground, has been made easier by large areas of bare peat, but since 2011 many of these have been sown with new heather.

2011, the repositioned debris from the impact point, looking back along the line of flight to the now-seeded bank, the true impact site

Indeed, the mound where the initial impact occurred had been cleared of debris in order to re-seed it, the repositioned debris having been deposited 65 feet short of the main terminal site, the tertiary pool remaining 200 feet beyond that in a small hollow, the three sites giving a post-impact track of 226°M.

The main terminal site, 2011

The tertiary site, 2011

In poor visibility reversing the outbound route would serve, but the shortest way (0.91 miles, 1.5 km) would be to progress on 164°M, passing to the west – to the right – of the TV enclosure (regardless of which summit parking area is used, this side gives far easier going!), knowing that the Woodhead Road is there as a backstop.

The crash site of Swordfish P4223 (see Section 15, below) is to be found at the head of Heyden Brook, leaving the path where it turns aside to cross the brook (as approached from the TV mast), and proceeding just 125 yards further along the main gully, on a heading of 288°M.

Most walkers in this area will also be taking in Black Hill, 650 yards from the brook crossing at Heyden Head on a heading of 266°M. An unashamed word of caution, therefore, for first-time visitors: Black Hill has an extensive and essentially convex summit, so before leaving it, and regardless of the visibility, determine the required direction of travel using any method bar 'instinct'.

15. Fairey Swordfish Mk.1 P4223
Heydon Head, Black Hill

SE 08338 04762 570 m

Unit and Squadron: No. 751 Squadron, Royal Naval Air Service Ford (Littlehampton), West Sussex

Date: 25 January 1940

Crew: pilot, killed

- Sub-Lieutenant Gerald Vyvian Williamson, Royal Naval Volunteer Reserve

Fairey Swordfish

For a single-engined, carrier-borne aircraft the Swordfish was surprisingly large, enhancing its short-landing and take-off capabilities with leading-edge slats and lift-augmenting ailerons. Its normal crew complement was three, but on 25 January 1940, when four new aircraft were to be ferried to Royal Naval Air Station Ford from No.22 Maintenance Unit at RAF Silloth, on the Solway Firth, only pilots were detailed for the task. Considering the time of year, however, it could well be that when Sub-Lieutenant Gerald Vyvian Williamson and three other Swordfish pilots set out from Ford to collect the machines, their non-involved crew members, whose own airborne positions were exposed to the airflow, were only too glad to wave their pilots god-speed on the odyssey that would culminate in a chilly three-hundred-mile delivery flight.

Just over a third of the way into that southbound flight, however, those formating realised that Sub-Lieutenant Williamson was no longer holding station. Not that this was a matter for undue concern, for although new to the Senior Service, Sub-Lieutenant Williamson had ten years of flying experience behind him; indeed he had been one of the 4,000 Britons holding flying licences (and 35,000 without!) who had applied to join the Civil Air Guard in July 1938. Moreover, as a founder member of the Yorkshire Light Aeroplane Club he was well acquainted not only with local winter flying conditions but the region where he had been missed. Except that he never did arrive back at RNAS Ford.

Indeed, nothing more was to be heard of him for a full month until, on 13 March 1940, Mr John Davies, later of Railway Cottages, Crowden, while clearing snow on the Woodhead-Holme Moss road (the A6024), was struck by an unfamiliar object silhouetted on the skyline, and decided to investigate. As he told researcher Mr John Ownsworth in 1970, his curiosity took him up a two-mile lift of icy moor towards Heydon Head, there to discover the wreckage of the missing Swordfish; and the corpse of Sub-Lieutenant Williamson, still firmly locked into the safety straps.

During Mr Davies' climb the weather had begun to deteriorate, but undaunted by this, if somewhat unsettled by his macabre discovery, the road-mender then made a Homeric trek through what became blizzard conditions down to the George and Dragon public house on the Woodhead Road, and the nearest telephone.

As the hours passed, the storm intensified, so that when Mr Harry Shaw, then the incumbent of the Fleece Inn, Holme, led an RAF recovery-cum-salvage detachment to the scene, conditions had become hazardous.

Nor did they improve. In fact, as evening approached and the eight men still engaged on the salvage element of the task had not returned, Mr Shaw organised a search party. Only it was to be well into the next day before the men were located on Sliddens Moss, having become disorientated and headed ever deeper into the moors rather than towards the nearby Holme Moss road and their transport. It was with great relief, therefore, that they were led down to Woodhead, and thence to Holmfirth, where two of the eight had to be hospitalised with frostbite.

As it was, even those who had not been frostbitten were to spend a full five days recuperating in Holmfirth's Victoria Hotel before being permitted to return to the moor and complete their task of reducing the wreckage.

The aim of burning and burying what debris it was not feasible to remove was to obviate its taking the attention of future search aircraft. Except that things buried in peat tend to surface – so that barely eighteen months later a Lysander pilot, injured and trapped in wreckage some three miles to the west, would watch in frustration as a searching machine persistently circled over the Swordfish site (See Lysander V9403, Section 8 above).

The investigation determined that Sub-Lieutenant Williamson had crashed some seventeen miles east of his planned track, and there being no evidence of mechanical malfunction, found that he had simply flown into cloud-covered ground.

There was still a fair amount of debris at the crash site in 2013, a site overlooked these many years by a television mast frequently lost within clouds of the sort which seemingly ensnared the sub-lieutenant. But then the numerous groughs lacing this moorland summit tend to hide the spot from all but the most serious searcher. And so, despite its proximity to both a major Black Hill footpath and the Holme Moss road, the site retains a certain stark forlornness.

Yet how much more forlorn it must have been during that lonely, sightless, and unseeing vigil back in January 1940, when long chill nights succeeded foreshortened icy days throughout the rigour of a winter month, and not a living soul strayed by!

Wies White at the Swordfish site, showing the Holme Moss aerial

VISITING THE SITE

The route to Heyden Head, a thirty minute, near-mile walk from the Holme Moss parking areas, is detailed in Section 14, above. From where the path crosses Heyden Brook (at SE 08448 04733 561 m), the Swordfish site is just 125 yards further up the gully on a heading of 288°M.

The nearest crash site to this, that of Sabre 19234, lies off path and some 785 yards from the stream crossing on a heading of 058°M.

16. Gloster Meteors FMk.8 WA791 and VZ518
Sliddens Moss, south-west of Black Hill

SE 06655 02900 506 m, starboard aircraft's impact point

SE 06705 02916 506 m, port aircraft's impact point

SE 06866 02923 503 m, major gulley site

SE 07161 02923 492 m, port aircraft's terminal site

SE 07140 02883 492 m, starboard aircraft's terminal site.

The terminal site is 540 yards from the initial impact point on a heading of 092°M

Unit and Squadron: No. 66 Squadron, RAF Linton-on-Ouse (north-west of York), No. 12 Group, Fighter Command

Date: 12 April 1951

Crew: two pilots, both killed:

- Flight Lieutenant David Merryweather Leach, formation leader (WA791)
- Flying Officer Anthony Hauxwell (VZ518)

A Meteor pair

It was in the Meteor's heyday as a first-line fighter, on 12 April 1951, that Flight Lieutenant David Leach, of No. 66 Squadron, was detailed to exercise four Meteor FMk.8s in practice air-combat manoeuvres at 30,000 feet. This was a standard fighter training sortie and would have involved the four dividing into the loosely-formating pairs in which they would hone their tactical skills. In order to get best value out of the exercise the machines had cine-cameras linked to their gun mechanisms so that the likely outcomes of their dummy attacks could be critically assessed after the sortie.

Although routine, and despite strict orders dictating the rules of engagement in such exercises – the nearest thing there was to real aerial combat – risk was inherent. And on this occasion, having led his foursome up through the intermediate-level cloud in a zigzagging, follow-my-leader, 'snake climb', Flight Lieutenant Leach found thick upper cloud baulking his purpose. Accordingly, in view of the unfavourable conditions, he aborted the cine-gun practice and directed his two sections to return to base, heading north-eastwards as independent pairs, each section to utilise the remaining sortie time in carrying out instrument flying and recovery procedures.

A short time later Flight Lieutenant Leach, now leading just Flying Officer Anthony Hauxwell, made a broadcast call that he had sighted Leeds through a gap and that he was commencing descent. In fact, backtracking events, he seems to have seen Stockport, for despite a distance-devouring descent through at least twenty thousand feet of cloud towards Linton, the dive took the pair into the 1,600 feet-above-sea-level Sliddens Moss, still some twenty-one miles short of Leeds. There was no fire, but the impact killed both pilots as their aircraft disintegrated in a 540-yard wing-to-wing debris trail.

That both aircraft should fly into the ground in such a manner might be wondered at, and certainly, while actually practising combat manoeuvres the pair would have flown a loose tactical formation that allowed each to look around and provide cover for the other. However, when descending through such a substantial cloud layer the formating pilot would be tucked in close, his only function being to religiously hold station, leaving the navigation and terrain clearance entirely to his leader.

It is an efficient method of penetrating cloud in company, but in the event of a mishap it is likely to be a case of lose one, lose both. Indeed, No. 66 Squadron was to experience another such loss three years later when, having re-equipped with Sabres, another of its pairs spread a debris trail between the heights of Kinder Scout and the depths of Black Ashop Moor (See *High Peak Air Crash Sites, Central Region*, page 17).

The board of inquiry had no option but to hold the leader to blame. For he had undisputedly led his section down to 1,600 feet, demonstrably below the safety height even had he been where he thought he was (when the safety height would still have been some 2,000 feet), let alone the safety height where he actually was, of 3,800 feet.

In 2013 this appeared to be one crash site where, despite the efforts of the original recovery team, the lapse of time, and the attentions of souvenir hunters, a substantial amount of debris seemed likely to remain for many years, not gathered into a particular pool, but still strung out in dual trails across the tufted, still largely trackless, expanse of Sliddens Moss.

Tailplane debris

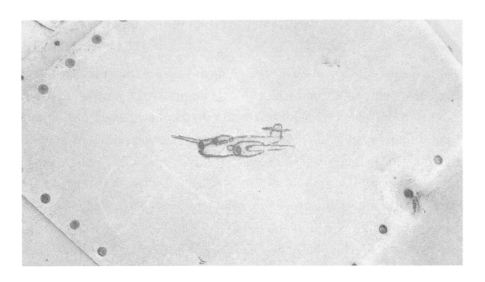

Detail on panel: Meteor sketch

A major debris pool near the terminal impact point

VISITING THE SITE

The two most convenient ways of reaching this site are from the car parks at Crowden, to the south, and Holme Moss Summit, to the north.

From Crowden (SK 07258 99266 213 m) the route passes the Outdoor Centre, then angles uphill to join the northerly-running Pennine Way. Over the course of an hour or so (2.28 miles) the track gradually climbs to afford the most splendid of rim walks with Crowden Great Brook rising from the depths to the right. The crossing to Sliddens Moss is conveniently made where a minor stream joins the brook at SE 06162 02999, at 463 metres. (Just 0.61 miles further on is the crash site of a Junkers Ju88 on Tooleyshaw Moss: see No-Surface-Debris sites, Section 16, below). After crossing the brook, any convenient route over the grassland will do, but a faint trail has been worn which heads for the extended crash site. Even should that trail be missed, the coarse moorland cover, tending more to cotton grass than the tussock variety, allows reasonably easy walking.

The second suggested route, starting at the Holme Moss Summit parking area (SE 07965 03898 516 m), follows the trail to Black Hill, then joins the paved Pennine Way to run south-west to the Crowden Great Brook crossing point used above (SE 06162 02999 463 m).

It is perfectly possible to walk the near one and a half miles off-path direct from Black Hill, or less strenuously, from Heyden Head, options many walkers might choose. Whatever the routing used, from the dual initial-impact points in the west the parallel debris trails reflect the stations kept by the formating aircraft, running easterly for some 540 yards.

The most straightforward return to the Holme Moss parking area would retrace the chosen outward route. The same applies to reversing the Crowden routing described. However, in this case there is also the new trail mentioned above. Yet another Crowden-bound variant runs eastwards and down the shoulder of Meadow Clough bound for Crowden Little Brook, the shoulder routing being recommended, for while Meadow Clough itself contains three waterfalls which are well worth seeing, negotiating the lower one in particular is more for rock climbers than walkers. Having crossed

Crowden Little Brook, a wide track, some feet above the stream, follows it for almost two miles to SK 07278 99753 303 m, at which point a footpath branches off to the right to descend to Crowden.

17. Handley Page Hampden Mk.1 L4055
Holme, Round Hill

SE 09958 05715 394 m

Unit and Squadron: No. 83 Squadron, RAF Scampton (north of Lincoln), No. 5 Group, Bomber Command

Date: 23 May 1940

Crew: four, all killed:

- Sergeant Stanley William Jenkins, pilot
- Sergeant Peter Josse, observer
- Aircraftman William Thornton, wireless operator
- Sergeant Alan Marsh, air gunner

Handley Page Hampden Mk.1

When war broke out in September 1939 the Handley-Page Hampden quickly ran into trouble as a day bomber, with five out of eleven reconnoitring Hampdens being shot down during just one encounter in that first month. Understandably, the type was quickly transferred to night bombing; the task Sergeant Stanley Jenkins and his crew had been engaging in, when, in the pre-dawn of 23 May 1940, their Hampden bomber was flown into Round Hill, above the village of Holme.

The crew were returning from raiding the German rail network at Mönchen-Gladbach, west of Düsseldorf. Yet in that early-war period of disillusional trial and error for both the planners and the aircrews of the RAF, such a night operation must surely have aimed to mildly disrupt rather than to cause substantial damage. Certainly it had not aspired to act as a meaningful interdiction measure against the German armies even then closing in around Dunkirk. Indeed, the harsh reality was that Hampden L4055 had accomplished no operational purpose whatsoever, because, unable to find a worthwhile legitimate target in Germany, Sergeant Jenkins had brought his bomb load back with him – it was, after all, very early in the war!

Compounding the situation for the crew, in the hours since the No. 83 Squadron force had departed from RAF Scampton, the weather in Lincolnshire had deteriorated below operating limits; accordingly the returning bombers were diverted to RAF stations in Norfolk. Regrettably, Sergeant Jenkins did not receive the diversion message, although brief contact was made with his aircraft when it was interrogated on coasting-in over Skegness.

Backplotting from the Holme crash site on a straight-line track to Mönchen-Gladbach – a routing not unlikely at that early stage of the war – it would seem that Sergeant Jenkins had actually passed overhead his Scampton base; only the speed of the along-track wind must have changed with the deterioration of weather because he overshot Scampton by fifty-five miles, a substantial error, although representing just twelve minutes in a one-hour-twenty-five-minute return leg.

That lapse time, however, during which the crew would have been assiduously searching for a pinpoint, took them over the high ground of the Peak District, and having let down to 1,300 feet – safe enough had they indeed been over flat, largely sea-level Lincolnshire – they flew directly into Round Hill where much of their bomb load exploded, the impact, the explosion, and the resulting fire, killing all four of them.

The explosion shattered the peace of sleeping Holme. Mr Derek Noble, for example, remembered that his mother sprang from her bed so hastily that she sprained her ankle; only to be disturbed again, even as she bathed the damaged member, by a thunderous knocking on the door as farmer Jack Gill of Lane Head Farm (the erstwhile Peacock Inn) arrived at a run.

'They're coming! They're coming!' he yelled, all the invasion-alarm rumours taking shape in his mind. ('Yes – *that* was my brother,' Mr John Gill, a more recent incumbent smiled fondly.)

An Air-Raid Precautions warden, Mrs Doris Haigh, was one of those earliest on the scene, but found that nothing could be done; indeed, until first light sheer discretion forced her to shelter behind a drystone wall as ammunition from the burning aircraft zipped around her.

The wreckage was left on the site for some months before being cleared, but in the interim those bombs which had not been detonated on impact were exploded by a bomb-disposal team. The crater this left was still visible in 2013, but although enough debris was detected to verify the terminal point, the crater was the only surface evidence of the crash. Apart, that is, from the wall through which the aircraft ploughed, although this had long since fallen into so ruinous a state as to afford meagre shelter from the winds; let alone from exploding 0.303-inch calibre machine-gun ammunition.

The impact site, with the A6024 Woodhead-Holmfirth Road descending from Holme Moss

2010, debris, on rucksack. Later secreted in drystone wall

Crater formed during bomb-disposal operations, with initial impact point beyond

VISITING THE SITE

Holme village lies on the A6024 Holmfirth-Woodhead Road to the north of Holme Moss. After leaving the A6024 and entering the village square, the road to the right (issuing at SE 10786 05952 305 m) passes the school, beyond which opportunity parking may be found. Taking two left-fork turns as they come gives access to Issues Road (more a track). After 300 yards a further left fork, at SE 10149 06274 346 metres, leads down Cliff Road (another track) to Round Hill. After a further 627 yards (at SE 09912 05768 386 m) and having negotiated a bend, the crash site is directly abeam to the left, by the drystone wall at SE 09958 05714, at 386 metres.

After an initial researching visit in 2003, the debris found was deposited in the wall. By 2013 only scraps were to be found while the drystone wall itself, as evidenced by photo-matching, was in very much worse repair and had lost a good two feet in height. The crater, however, was still very evident although a non-related hollow some yards further along the track, had been filled in.

Having come that far, any walker might consider it worthwhile continuing to the footpath at SE 09659 05591, 429 metres – not shown on the map –, and following the spine upwards onto the moor for five or ten minutes to take advantage of the spectacular view.

Barnsley Area

18. Armstrong Whitworth Whitley Mk.5, Z9289
Pogmoor, Barnsley (western Barnsley)

SE 33135 066580 142 m

Unit and Station: No. 102 Squadron, RAF Dalton

(south of Thirsk, Yorkshire), No. 4 Group, Bomber Command

Date: 6 January 1942

Occupants: five, two killed, one injured, two uninjured:

- Sergeant Alexander Hollingworth, Royal Australian Air Force, pilot, killed
- Sergeant John Toker Clough Hazeldine, RAF, second pilot, parachuted successfully
- Sergeant Ed A. Brain, Royal Canadian Air Force (RCAF), observer, parachuted successfully
- Flight Sergeant Alexander Gibson Buchanan, RCAF, wireless operator/air gunner, killed
- Sergeant Leonard Jackson, RAF, air gunner (rear), parachuted, injuring ankle

Cherbourg's dock installations targeted

At 0424 hours on 6 January 1942, Whitley Z9289 got airborne from RAF Dalton, near Thirsk, Yorkshire, as part of a Whitley force tasked to raid dock installations and shipping at Cherbourg. Encountering total cloud cover over the target, Sergeant Alexander Hollingworth, an Australian attached to No. 102 Squadron, and on his first operation as a captain, decided to abort the sortie. While still over the target, however, the starboard power plant malfunctioned in a manner which precluded the propeller being feathered to reduce the drag, so that the aircraft, a type with poor enough performance even with both engines giving full power, was unable to maintain altitude. Despite this, having crossed the Channel, rather than setting down at the first available airfield, Sergeant Hollingworth elected to hold a course for RAF Dalton, still some 240 miles distant – for the Whitley, at best, over a hour and forty minutes flying time away!

The aircraft continued to lose height even though, twelve miles short of Sheffield, the bombs were made safe and jettisoned onto moorland. But then, at 1005 hours, on approaching the south-western outskirts of Barnsley – and by now at a reportedly *very* low level! – the heavily put-upon starboard engine caught fire, its propeller first windmilling, then overspeeding. The vastly increased drag this runaway condition caused, together with the associated raising of the critical handling speed, effectively rendered the aircraft uncontrollable.

Three crew members baled out successfully, all three landing close together in the Broadway area, if with Sergeant Jackson injuring an ankle on landing. Flight Sergeant Buchanan, though, jumping altogether too low was killed when he struck the railway lines, barely a quarter of a mile further on. Sergeant Hollingworth himself had no time to jump as the aircraft dived into, and exploded in, Phase Quarry, just yards beyond the railway, and closer still to Cresswell Street, Pogmoor.

In September 1985 the erstwhile observer – navigator – Ed Brain, recalled that return flight.

'Jacko Jackson, the rear gunner, and I had been lent to Bruno Hollingworth as this was his first op as a captain. Leaving Cherbourg we'd set our IFF to Emergency so as we crossed the English coast one of three searchlights laid down its beam towards the nearest 'drome. I have to say that when Bruno eyed it, and said, "They want us to land, but I want to make it back to base," no-one disagreed. From then on, as we stooged slowly up England, everyone was busy. I maintained the plot, getting bearings from Buck Buchanan and pinpoints from Jacko, and advising of the airfields we passed. For Bruno kept going. Later, as we sank lower, I double-checked that the bombs were safe before jettisoning them. But not that long afterwards Bruno punched me on the arm and pointed to where fifteen-foot flames were streaming back from the starboard engine. As he was off intercom, I told everyone to abandon. Johnny Hazeldine went, and Jacko, I assumed, but Buck Buchanan I found scrabbling inside his wireless set. I grabbed his leg, and when he realised what was going on, led him towards the nose. Bruno had no parachute, and would clearly have to ride it out, but although we exchanged a thumbs-up his face was ashen. I saw Buck go, then the airflow took away one of my flying boots. After which I can remember little, only that I rolled out of a very unstable descent into a safe landing. Buck, though didn't make it.'

Mr and Mrs Trevor and Carol Stockdale, of Cresswell Street, were able to verify the impact area and affirmed that, the quarry-pit notwithstanding, debris was widespread. At the same time another Cresswell Street resident, Mrs Kitty Moss (née Goodyear), at a hale ninety years, readily recalled the crash itself.

'I was scrubbing my front step,' she said, 'when I saw this bomber coming down. It was almost vertical, and it was trailing fire and smoke, and I saw a parachute over towards Broadway. I knew my mother was in, so I ran down, and round the corner, to her place.' She pointed across the street. 'At the time,' she explained, 'there were two terraces, separated by a gap where the garages are today. Mum's house was on the right of the gap. The plane crashed where the playing field is now, and although no houses were damaged, a wing landed in the gap. Then the police arrived, and the RAF lads, who very soon took everything away.' She smiled. 'Mum always used to say, "He were a good man that pilot, for if he'd flown down with his wings level he'd have destroyed the terraces on each side. As it was, by coming down vertically, he missed them both.'"

The RAF court of inquiry, understandably, was censorious of Sergeant Hollingworth's judgment in pressing on rather than putting down at the first of the many available airfields he had overflown. The technical malfunction, it found, had been caused by the failure of a component crucial to propeller-pitch control.

Former Sergeant Brain, resumed his account. 'Next day Jacko and I were asked if we felt fit to fly, and when we said we did, we took part in a flour-bag attack on the airfield with our own crew. After which it was back to normal. Johnny Hazeldine's next op, though, on 26 January, was to Emden, his first in command, only he never came back. And later, on 24 September 1942, after I had finished my tour, Jacko too was lost on ops. For my part, after being screened I became an Oboe instructor and operator, sitting on the ground and telling Mosquitoes when to drop their bombs. After D Day we moved to Europe, so that I finished the war in Germany, returning to Canada as a squadron leader.'

By 2012 the tragedy, one of the very few in this series which occurred in the course of an actual Bomber Command operation, was commemorated by a tasteful plaque on the wall of a British-Legion-owned bungalow not that many yards from the filled-in-quarry impact point.

Mrs Kitty Moss, the gap, and the impact site

The memorial plaque

VISITING THE SITE

There is parking to be found in the Cresswell Street area, and while the quarry impact site is now playing fields, the plaque is still to be seen.

Whitley

Sergeant Alexander Hollingworth

Sergeant Ed Brain

PART TWO – SITES WITH NO SURFACE DEBRIS

Each of these sites has been proven by metal-detector search – most showing positive traces of aircraft material – while others have been identified by photographs and witness testimony, an example of each being shown.

Top left, an identifiable component, in this instance from a 1919 DH9A, now in a private collection. Right, witness testimony, in this case erstwhile shepherd Tom Adlington at a Wellington crash site. Bottom, photographic evidence, illustrated by a Blenheim crash on Woolley Flats, Glossop.

Oldham

1. Handley Page Heyford K4874
Dingle Farm, Moorside, Oldham

SD 94939 08465 226 m

Unit and Squadron: No. 102 Squadron, RAF Finningley (near Doncaster), No. 3 Group, Bomber Command

Date: 12 December 1936

Crew: four crew, three injured:

- Flight Lieutenant Charles Patrick Villiers, pilot
- Observer, presently unidentified, uninjured
- Leading Aircraftman John Mackan, wireless operator
- Leading Aircraftman Donald J.M. Keys, air gunner

Handley Page Heyford

Heyfords in formation

On Saturday, 12 December 1936, a markedly foggy day, seven Handley Page Heyford bombers of No. 102 (Ceylon) Squadron, having completed a detachment to Ulster, were detailed to return in formation to their home station of RAF Finningley – Robin Hood airport, since 2005 –, near Doncaster, in Yorkshire. Prior to their departure from RAF Aldergrove (subsequently Belfast International) they were updated on the weather pattern in the mainland, where widespread fog and ice had led to chaotic conditions which were now exacerbated by snow; such a conjunction of fog and heavy snow storms being indicative of very significant wind changes aloft.

The detachment leader, Squadron Leader Attwood, planned to return in a loose Vic formation – the Heyford being renowned for its stability in formation – initially aiming for the shortest sea crossing, of 115 miles to Barrow, then steering directly for Finningley, some 110 miles further on. Nevertheless, and particularly in view of the weather, each pilot and observer (navigator) would have produced a flight plan for their own aircraft against the not unlikely event that they became detached from the formation.

By all accounts, the plan went well as far as the Barrow landfall. After that, however, the weather seems to have been even worse than anticipated, and things began to go awry. The full story of the other six machines is recounted in the southern book of this High Peak series (Section 35, Sites with No Surface Debris), but some time later people on the ground at Moorside, to the north of Oldham, became aware that an aircraft – Heyford K4874, it would transpire, piloted by Flight Lieutenant Charles Villiers – was circling in the clouds above them. The engine roar reverberated downwards for a good thirty minutes, during which time it became evident that the pilot was unable to find a break in the clouds wide enough to show him the ground. It would also have indicated to the initiated, that, having become uncertain of his position, the pilot was not about to take the chance of descending blind. It is likely too, in view of the general weather pattern, that his aircraft was collecting a substantial amount of profile-spoiling ice on its lifting surfaces, leading to doubts about its continued controllability. The time came, therefore, when Flight Lieutenant Villiers gave the order to abandon, his three crew members taking to their parachutes in disciplined fashion.

Deservedly, the abandonment itself went well. Just the same, Leading Aircraftman John Mackan, the wireless operator, landed on a mill roof, and having divested himself of his parachute the better to slide further down, fell through a skylight and had to be hospitalised with a badly cut hand. For his part, Flight Lieutenant Villiers alighted on the roof of a cottage; and then fell off, breaking his leg. Another crew member, Leading Aircraftman Donald J.M. Keys, also had to be hospitalised with head injuries. The observer, however, presently unidentified, came to earth safely in the middle of a football field.

Their abandoned Heyford, left to its own devices, lost height and crashed only yards from Dingle Farm, near Besom Hill Reservoir, impacting heavily and burning out. Press photographs of the burnt-out machine are graphic, but the fair prints have been disposed of and the extant copies are too blurred to usefully reproduce. Significantly, the aircraft, while only twelve miles off track, was forty miles short of Finningley when it crashed.

The whole incident represented a debacle of the first order; but it was a setback from which lessons could be learnt, and one which spurred on the development of de-icing systems on large aircraft. Nor did it adversely affect Flight Lieutenant Villiers' career, for he emerged from the Second World War as a wing commander.

Rather remarkably, local awareness of the accident has proved long-lived; accordingly, Mr Walter Taylor, of Button Hole, was able to point out the site where the aircraft had impacted and burnt out. 'Dad and I', he explained, standing at the impact site only yards from the heaped stones which alone marked the erstwhile Dingle Farm, 'knew the place well, for being coal merchants we delivered here every day.' He paused, and indicated the spread of the town beyond. 'At that time there were scores upon scores of mill chimneys belching smoke in Oldham alone, so our fogs were actually smogs, even cutting out the daylight on occasion. And visibility was particularly bad that day. This large aeroplane had been circling for some time before it crashed, but with Dad knowing his way so well, despite the fog, he was able to run directly from Button Hole to where it had come down. Fortunately the plane had missed the farmhouse and piled up into this drystone wall. But it soon became clear to Dad that none of the crew had been on board, and that there was nothing he could do. I believe he got some maps from it, however, and something else, although the police took that away [local belief had it that this was the aircraft's Very signal pistol.] There was little enough left of the plane, though. And eventually that was dragged away. Now even the farm's gone.'

VISITING THE SITE

From Oldham's Moorside, the visitor should turn off Grains Road (at SD 94430 08920) into Mark Lane, following this to the furthest extent then parking where convenient. There is a public footpath, but basically the site of the crash (SD 94939 08465 226 m) lies some 300 yards further away on a heading of 162°M. Only some tumbled stones remain of Dingle Farm.

The coordinates relevant to the other aircraft concerned are:

K4868, SJ 96785 84713 243 m Homestead Farm, Disley, Cheshire

K6898, SJ 96805 84619 197 m The Homestead, Disley, Cheshire

Mr Walter Taylor of Buttonhole at the crash site of Heyford K4874

Stalybridge Area

2. Unidentified Type, Crows i' th' Wood, Stamford Moor Golf Club, Stalybridge

SD 97768 00700 160 m, Hole 5, 'Oakfield'.

Operator: unknown

Date: 6 March 1918

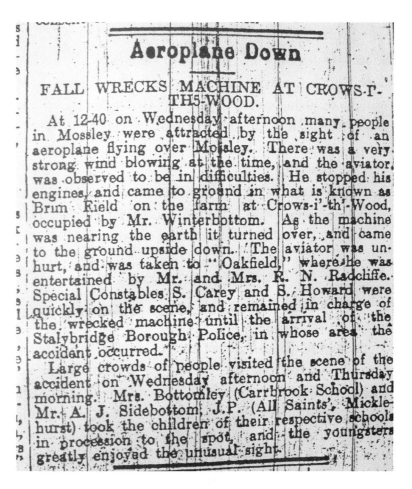

Aeroplane Down

FALL WRECKS MACHINE AT CROWS-I'-TH5-WOOD.

At 12-40 on Wednesday afternoon many people in Mossley were attracted by the sight of an aeroplane flying over Mossley. There was a very strong wind blowing at the time, and the aviator was observed to be in difficulties. He stopped his engines, and came to ground in what is known as Brun Field on the farm at Crows-i'-th'-Wood, occupied by Mr. Winterbottom. As the machine was nearing the earth it turned over, and came to the ground upside down. The aviator was unhurt, and was taken to " Oakfield," where he was entertained by Mr. and Mrs. R. N. Radcliffe. Special Constables S. Carey and S. Howard were quickly on the scene, and remained in charge of the wrecked machine until the arrival of the Stalybridge Borough Police, in whose area the accident occurred.

Large crowds of people visited the scene of the accident on Wednesday afternoon and Thursday morning. Mrs. Bottomley (Carrbrook School) and Mr. A. J. Sidebottom, J.P. (All Saints', Micklehurst) took the children of their respective schools in procession to the spot, and the youngsters greatly enjoyed the unusual sight.

The **Stalybridge Reporter** *article, 6 March 1918*

On Saturday 9 March 1918, the *Stalybridge Reporter* recorded that on 6 March an aeroplane had crashed at Crows i' th' Wood Farm. No details of the aircraft are supplied, only that it flew over Mossley at 1240 hours when 'the aviator was observed to be in difficulties' owing to the strong wind. Accordingly, the account records, 'he stopped his engines' and came down in Brun Field, at Mr Winterbottom's Crows i' th' Wood Farm [locals say Crozzitwood]. However, at very low level the machine was turned over by the turbulence and struck the ground inverted. Notwithstanding, the aviator was unhurt and was taken to, and entertained at, 'Oakwood' [in fact, Oakfields House], then the home of Mr and Mrs R.N. Radcliffe.

The account describes how, during that Wednesday afternoon and the Thursday morning, the Stalybridge Police controlled the large crowds who came to sightsee, giving special mention of Miss Bottomley, of Carrbrook School, and Mr A.J. Sidebottom, JP, of All Saints' School, Micklehurst, who took their pupils 'in procession to the spot' where 'the youngsters greatly enjoyed the unusual sight'.

One might, perhaps, think that aeroplanes were no longer all that very much of a novelty so late in the First World War, but then most aerial activity would have been well to the south of the country.

VISITING THE SITE

The upset occurred on ground now occupied by Hole No. 5 on the Stamford Golf Course, just off the A635, to the south of Mossley. The present course, in fact, grew from the nine-hole Crows i' th' Wood course, Hole No.5, an original hole from that course, still retaining its original identity of Oakfield. Oakfield House is now the Clubhouse, but no record of the crash is held by the club.

This intriguing early incident came to light through the diligence of researcher Mr Alan Jones, of Stalybridge.

Hole 5, Crows i' th' Wood

Oldfield House

3. Avro Avian Mk.3 G-EBVZ
Hough Hill, Stalybridge

SJ 96284 97461 192 m

Operator: Lancashire Aero Club, Woodford

Date: 25 March 1928

Occupants: two, both survived:

- Miss Winifred Sawley Brown, pilot, slight cut on chin
- Mr Walter Samuel Browning, passenger, film salesman, private pilot, unhurt

Spectators involved: Six children and a young woman; one child killed:

- Master Jack (Jackie) Humphrey Hood, 7, killed, severe head injuries
- Miss Edith Hood, 13, head wound and shock
- Miss Mary Taylor, 7, injuries to arm
- Master Harry Downend, 14, slight head wound
- Master William Brown, 8, injuries to left foot
- Master James Poynter, 7, injury to left leg
- Miss Margaret Walmsy, 17, shock

Miss Winifred Brown with her Avian

The Avro Avian was a light sporting aircraft designed for long-range races and used to good effect by such celebrated fliers as Amelia Earhart and Bert Hinkler, but also by Mrs Emily-Lynn (Lady Mary Heath) who used the type for her record-setting Cape Town to London flight.

Another aviatrix to favour the Woodford-built Avian – hers was a birthday gift from her father – was Miss Winifred Sawley Brown, of Cheshire. In July 1930 Miss Brown was to beat all her male competitors (to 'actually' beat them, as a contemporary source had it) and win the prestigious King's Cup Air Race. This win, which drew praise from the world-famous Miss Earhart herself, entailed flying a 750-mile route around England, a feat which Miss Brown accomplished at an average speed of 102.7 miles an hour, winning comfortably, as the same source observes, 'by consistent rather than spectacular flying'.

But then perhaps Miss Brown had tasted to the full the bitterness inherent in any flying bordering on the spectacular after an incident which had occurred on Sunday, 25 March 1928, almost two years before her King's Cup triumph.

At that time Miss Brown, an international hockey star who had served with the Red Cross during the First World War, had already been among the foremost of Britain's women aviators – only the week before, at Croydon Aerodrome, she had been presented to reform-minded King Amanullah Kahn, of recently-independent Afghanistan. On that fatal Sunday, however, she became embroiled in an infamously-mishandled publicity stunt in which a young boy was killed and five other children and a young woman of seventeen injured. Miss Brown was exonerated from all blame by the inquest jury; nonetheless, the trauma was evidently deep-seated.

The stunt had been conceived by Mr Milton W. Parker, the manager of the *New Prince's Cinema*, Stalybridge, to promote his premises by having a copy of the new First World War film, *What Price Glory?* flown from Woodford Aerodrome to a local venue. A film salesman, Mr Walter Samuel Browning, who, as a member of the Lancashire Aero Club, held a pilot's 'A' Licence (the modern Private Pilot's Licence), vetted the proposed venue – a field near Hunters' Tower, then a singular landmark on the Gorse Hall Estate at Hough Hill, Stalybridge –, and having confirmed its suitability, agreed to do the job. Accordingly, publicity arrangements were made which promised that after delivery the aircraft would 'engage in manoeuvres similar to those used in actual warfare'. In addition numerous placards directed spectators, 'To the New Prince's Landing Ground'.

By the appointed time of two o'clock in the afternoon of the twenty-fifth, a foggy, virtually windless day, a crowd estimated at twenty thousand had gathered to view the spectacle. Only, ostensibly because of the fog, nothing happened. Eventually, however, at three-thirty the aeroplane appeared briefly, but then disappeared once more. And the waiting continued. Predictably, as the still-unexplained delay became yet more protracted, so the chilled crowd dwindled. Just the same, at shortly after four o'clock, when the aircraft came into sight once more and this time began to circle overhead, an estimated twelve thousand spectators still remained.

The venue was a roughly rectangular field, relatively narrow, and totally enclosed by drystone walls; indeed, running across the narrow 'stop end' to the north was a double wall, part of the 430-yard-long Victorian rifle range, the inner wall some four feet high; the far one, which also served as the Estate boundary, rising to seven feet. The crowd had gathered six-and-more deep along all the edging walls and many, despite 'Danger, Keep Out' notices and a Dukinfield Police Force presence, had clambered up to stand or sit on the walls themselves.

The foggy conditions, however, had not been the primary reason for the delay. In truth, this was due to the confusion which, unknown to the crowd, had reigned for some time at Woodford Aerodrome. Mr Browning, having made a reconnaissance flight in a club aeroplane earlier that day, had decided against attempting the delivery himself. But now the man who had elected to fly in his stead, a Mr Cantrill, seemed unaccountably engrossed in something else. In the face of which Miss Winifred Brown, who had arrived on a purely social visit to the flying club, was approached, and on being told that the delivery was urgent, readily agree to do the flight in her own aircraft, taking Mr Browning in the front seat as her passenger.

Mr Browning, not without ostentation, stowed the precious film container, but once airborne was unable to locate the site in the prevailing poor visibility. However, after returning to Woodford Aerodrome, and having studied the map once more, he'd had Miss Brown take off again when, on locating the field, she was 'astonished' to see such a crowd assembled. Yet to convey this astonishment was impossible, for as her passenger later testified, 'being in a hurry I could not be bothered to rig the earphones into my own helmet', so that while he could talk to Miss Brown, she could not reply. For that matter, when he asked her to 'put on a bit of a show', she discounted the request, and doubtfully eyeing the landing site through the mist, circled the field a number of times, assessing the problems it posed, and only then beginning a first, tentative, landing approach.

For as she, in turn, testified later, she was well aware that this was a field smaller than any she had ever attempted to land upon before. Further, it was one made yet more restrictive by the people craning upwards from the near-end wall, their presence immediately raising the height she would have to allow to clear the obstacle, at the same time effectively cutting down on the distance remaining available for the landing. Indeed, before actually touching down she was to make six more trial approaches, putting on power on each occasion and climbing away.

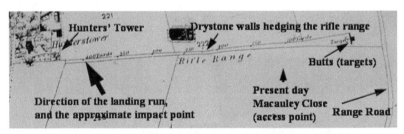

The since-demolished Hunters' Tower, and the Victorian Rifle Range

The Avian's line of approach towards the rifle-range wall

Clearly she could not afford to merely skim the people-studded wall on the approach, therefore, as she positioned herself for the final time, she gave her tyres a handsome margin. But this forced a late touchdown. Worse still, experiencing a dead calm near the surface, she floated even more and so was unable to put her brakeless wheels onto the ground until she was practically halfway into the already limiting field. Then, with throttle closed, and hardly a breath of headwind to slow her, she waited for the grass to retard the momentum of the machine. Only to realise, seconds later, that the speed was barely diminishing! Yet ahead of her loomed a double wall, and a further jam-packed line of spectators! As she later recorded, she momentarily considered swinging the aircraft – but to each side the spectators appeared to be thronging closer. So, as the only alternative, she put on full power and desperately heaved the nose skywards.

The spectators had already experienced a fair measure of the thrills they had anticipated, for during each trial approach the passenger had waved, at which 'they had cheered wildly, some throwing their hats into the air in excitement'. Now, as just yards from the crowd the power came on and the propeller blurred into a shining disk once more, they patently took to this to be part of the show. Indeed, one of those present, a Councillor Ashton, was later to testify, 'What surprised me was that the people did not move away. They must have thought the airplane was like a motor car with brakes, and that it could be brought to a standstill immediately.'

As it was, with no headwind to assist it, the machine could not develop sufficient lift and drove nose-high through the first wall to impact heavily upon the second.

Nose into the far wall ...

Tail draped over the near wall ...

Within moments, Miss Brown, her chin welling blood from a cut occasioned as her lap-strap snapped, was helped from the aeroplane by cinema staff and bundled away towards Hunters' Tower.

'Was anyone hurt?' she desperately asked those surrounding her.

'No', she was told. And only with that assurance, and having already seen her passenger scramble clear unaided, did she submit to having her chin attended to.

Only people *had* been hurt: six children and a young woman who had been sitting on the first wall and who had been unable to scramble out of the way; each of them injured, some by debris, some by the machine itself, albeit most only superficially hurt and all to be released from Ashton Infirmary immediately after treatment. But seven-year old Jack – Jackie – Hood had been killed outright, dying instantly – as the inquest would later be assured – from severe lacerations to the brain. So that his body, after being moved to a house near Hunters' Tower for examination by a doctor, was taken on to the mortuary at Dukinfield.

Back at the landing site a frenzy of excitement prevailed, with women pushing forwards to ascertain the identity of the injured youngsters, each fearing for their own, and with several of them fainting ...

The tragedy struck across the whole community, and not least at the Hob Hill Day School where, on the morning after the accident, 'even the little infants were impressed by the sadness of the occurrence ...' Where, also, the headmistress would remember that just days before, Jackie, as everyone knew him, had presented her with a pair of sprouting acorns, saying 'I've brought you two young oak trees …'

At the funeral service the next week the presiding clergyman, the Reverend V.R. Smeed, spoke out against the practices of advertising. 'We need', he fulminated, 'another commandment, "Six days shalt thou advertise, but on the seventh remember the Lord thy God".' Adding, in a voice that only too vainly echoes down the years, 'Even in advertising the canons of good taste should be observed.'

Miss Brown would later give the newspapers her, evidently shock-hazed impression of the final moments of her ill-fated landing attempt. As they quoted her: 'The whole affair is extremely regrettable, and I was horrified when I learnt the full extent of the tragedy. I had no intention whatever of flying when I went to Woodford on Sunday afternoon. On my arrival there I was told that it was a matter of the utmost urgency that Mr Browning should go to Stalybridge with certain films.'

She had therefore offered to make the flight in her machine, which was hangared at Woodford, and eventually made the fatal approach.

'I throttled down the engine, preparatory to landing, and under ordinary circumstances this, of course, would reduce the engine [aircraft] speed. The engine [aircraft], however, did not seem to slow down, and as I swept earthwards I saw a large crowd standing where I was about to land. There was only one thing to do to avoid the crowd, and I endeavoured to do it. I opened out the engine … and tried to rise. The next thing I knew was that the machine had struck the wall and was lying across it.'

She was further quoted as attributing her inability to slow down as 'due to the sheltered conditions created by the wall … an absence of wind, which is the only braking power when landing.'

Miss Winifred Brown displayed fine sensitivity by not attending the funeral, where her presence could only have caused distress and given rise to renewed newspaper interest. Her floral tribute, however, bearing the expression 'With deepest sympathy', spoke for the grief which superseded the horror of learning what had been so briefly hidden from her.

At the inquest on 7 April 1928, however, as recorded by the Stalybridge paper, *The Reporter*, it became obvious that this was not the only thing that been concealed from her.

Mr Browning, private pilot and film salesman, giving evidence before Mr J.A.K. Ferns, the District Coroner, initially described the incident as a 'piece of pure bad luck'. But he was not to get away so easily. The coroner listened as the witness explained that he had been unable to 'hear anything Miss Brown said, of course, on account of the roar of the machine, but as she circled so many times … [he] presumed she was doubtful about the desirability of landing in so small a field.'

Had Miss Brown, the coroner wanted to know, been told it was a small field surrounded by walls?

'I did not tell her,' Mr Browning replied blandly.

And when the coroner pressed, 'You seriously tell the jury that you considered a field 150 yards long on one side, and 190 on the other, and surrounded by stone walls, suitable for landing an aeroplane in?' Browning promptly asserted, 'I could have landed a machine there.'

Only to have the coroner snap, clearly referring to the original plan, under which Mr Browning would have been the pilot, 'Why didn't you?'

Following hard upon these exchanges Sergeant F. Wheatman of the Dukinfield Police Force supplied damning details of the landing site. From corner to corner along the landing approach was just 179 yards. From the point of the aeroplane's touchdown to the fatal wall was only 108 yards. The field was marked solely by a central white circle with white corner flags, and had no restraint against a surging crowd. Nor had any arrangement been made for signalling to the pilot from the ground.

But perhaps the most heinous aspect of the affair was yet to come out. For it transpired that the box carried in the aircraft by Mr Browning had been empty! That from the outset the intention had always been to deliver the film by road!

Miss Winifred Brown, questioned on this revelation, replied categorically, 'If I had thought it was an empty box I wouldn't have gone.'

Whereas Mr Browning, questioned in his turn, was almost patronising.

'It would have been *far* too dangerous to carry a celluloid film in an aeroplane.'

At which stage the coroner asked both the cinema manager and Mr Browning individually, 'So this was a publicity stunt to delude the public?' and 'A hoax on the public?' Receiving the answers, 'Precisely,' and, 'That is so. A publicity stunt.'

Such contrite admissions, however, did not save either from the coroner's acerbity. Tersely he sought and gained admissions that the salesman had never been a captain in the army, and had never been in the Royal Air Force (claims previously made, one must suppose). Also that he had little experience of landing aeroplanes other than at Woodford, with its spacious manoeuvring area. Following which the coroner once more addressed the jury, directing them to recognise that Miss Winifred Brown had had nothing to do with the scheme, indeed that she had been deliberately lied to concerning the film.

'You have seen Browning in the witness box,' he reminded the members. 'And you must judge for yourselves whether he is experienced enough for choosing a field.' After which he commented witheringly, 'I think his flying experience has been gained in an office but you might think otherwise …'

And outraged still by the revelation that the intention all along had been to delude the public, the jury reached their verdict, completely exonerating Miss Winifred Brown from all blame, and expressing their belief that she had done everything in her power to avoid a much more serious accident.

Horrific as the incident had been, and deeply as it had grieved her, the trauma had not irreparably blunted Miss Brown's zest for aviating. Indeed, as already seen, the following year, flying G-EBVZ once again, she entered the prestigious King's Cup Air Race, and as Amelia Earhart justifiably crowed in her 1932 book, became the only woman to have won it. Indeed, it would be 1981 – fifty-one years – before her exploit was emulated; while in the interim Miss Brown, as a winner, would have been the sole woman entitled to eat her annual celebratory dinners at the Royal Aero Club.

Nine years later, when war broke out in 1939, and despite having reached the age of forty, Miss Brown – Mrs Adams rather, for by then she had married Mr Ron Adams, her fiancé passenger in the King's Cup Air Race – might have seemed a prime contender for the Air Transport Auxiliary, the civil organisation which delivered aircraft from the factories to operational airfields. Instead, she turned to the sea, and served as a coxswain at the Saunders-Roe flying-boat base at Beaumaris, Anglesey.

Miss Winifred Brown

All those years earlier, at the 1928 inquest into the Stalybridge crash, the District Coroner, after consulting the attending Flight Lieutenant P.H. Davy of the Air Accidents Investigation Branch, had stressed the importance the Air Ministry attached to the inquiry, 'as affecting the safety of the public in the future in such cases as these.' A concern which is reflected in the stringent rules which have for so long been imposed upon all public flying displays.

By 2013 only vestigial evidence remained of even the site of the 1928 tragedy, for the drystone wall on the approach, over which Miss Brown had dared not merely skim, together with those on the sides of the field, had been demolished as housing estates proliferated, spreading, seemingly inexorably, from Stalybridge. Notwithstanding which, sections of the double wall of the rifle range still held back the urban flow. So it was that, although nothing remained to indicate the actual impact point, and no debris could have been expected, the spot could be deduced – as it has been here – by plotting out the known distances involved.

Beyond the bungalows and the remnants of the Victorian rifle-range walls a commendably active Local Trust, often fronted by its worthy representative Mr Graham Brown, capably preserved the Estate of the former Gorse Hall. The Hall was demolished in 1910, but was once the home of Beatrix Potter's grandmother where the young Beatrix spent several family holidays. Of more notoriety it was also the scene of the now celebrated unsolved Storrs murder of 1909. As for the area beyond the double walls upon which the attempted overshoot had foundered so tragically on that baleful day in 1928, that was regularly mown to provide, somewhat ironically perhaps, a safe, traffic-free playground for the local children.

Local historian Mr Graham Brown indicates the rifle-range's parallel walls

VISITING THE SITE

Visitors approaching from Stalybridge should leave the B6175 at SJ 95996 98248 and turn into Gorse Hall Drive, finding convenient parking. From the end of the Drive the area of the crash site lies 300 yards off on a heading of 178°M. Approaching from the south, permissive parking may be found in Macauley Drive (SJ 96461 97435). Entering from this direction gives immediate access to the parkland, the line of the double-walled Victorian Rifle Range, and the area of the crash site. Nothing is left, however, of Hunters' Tower.

3. Avro Anson Mk.1 DJ680
Hollingworth Hall Moor, north-west of Glossop

SJ 99700 97710 313 m

Unit and Squadron: No. 2 Pilots Advanced Flying Unit, RAF Millom
(Broughton-in-Furness), No. 25 Group, Flying Training Command
Date: 20 March 1944
Crew: five, all injured:

- Flight Sergeant H. Edward (Ted) Rimmer, pupil pilot, bruises and
  abrasions
- Pilot Officer N. Kerr, pupil navigator, ankles broken
- Flight Sergeant Alan Boyd, pupil wireless operator, bruises and
  abrasions
- Sergeant D.J. Mance, screen navigator, badly concussed, subsequently
  grounded
- Sergeant Jacobs, screen wireless-operator, bruises and abrasions

On 20 March 1944 Anson DJ680 was engaged in a night navigational
exercise when, at 0715 hours, in conditions of grudging first light, recently-
promoted Flight Sergeant Ted Rimmer found himself forced to accept that
he and his mainly-pupil crew were lost.

By that time they had been airborne for two and a quarter hours
on a route that had required them to fly from Cumbria's RAF Millom to
Anglesey and then to Stafford before returning to base. Throughout the
flight, however, thick rain-bearing clouds had hampered the navigator from
determining his position. At the same time the intense static generated
by these clouds had prevented the wireless operator from assisting with
either radio fixes or bearings. But with the fuel state reducing towards the
safe limit it became imperative that the aircraft's position be established,
and seeing no alternative, Flight Sergeant Rimmer made the decision to
descend below cloud.

Commencing his descent at 7,000 feet he eventually emerged into clear
air, only to find the ground obscured by a still lower cloud layer. Cautiously

edging yet further down, and with all available crew eyes alert for any surface feature that would afford a pinpoint, he re-entered cloud with 1,500 feet indicated on his altimeter; only to be faced, after descending for just a minute or two longer, with the loom of solid ground.

Desperately heaving back on the stick he managed to raise the nose and indeed, to match the upward-rising slope, for although the Anson bellied into the ground, its structure suffered only superficial damage. Nevertheless, the impact was violent enough to throw navigator, Pilot Officer Kerr, from the astrodome, causing him to break both his ankles, and to concuss the screen navigator, Sergeant Mance, who was thrown forwards into an obstruction.

Having evacuated the aircraft, and with his stranded crew as settled as could be expected, Flight Sergeant Rimmer had barely begun to take stock when, just visible through the rain and mist, he saw a providential light. This gave him some orientation, and after he had picked his way downhill in the slowly paling darkness, brought him to a cottage belonging to Landslow Green Farm – not the sole example of such bad blackout practices in the Peakland area! Here he raised the alarm, got aid for his injured crew members, and discovered that his aircraft had come to ground on Hollingworth Hall Moor, some seventy-five miles from its Millom base.

The impact area, looking towards Hollingworth Hall Farm

Later, Flight Sergeant Rimmer would recall that on reaching 1,000 feet on his altimeter he had expected to have at least that much clear air beneath him, for Millom, where the altimeter had been set, was at sea level. Except that Hollingworth Hall Moor stands at an altitude of some 1,050 feet above sea level.

The court of enquiry could not afford to be overly generous in its findings, the flight having been authorised at a minimum altitude of 2,500 feet, and accordingly the members held the captain, Flight Sergeant Rimmer, 'essentially to blame for the accident' in coming below that height. The summary of evidence then ordered against the flight sergeant (the normal precursor to a court martial) also found that he had been guilty of disobeying orders in descending below the safety height; but did concede that bad weather had played a part. As a result the case was eventually dealt with at a lower level than court martial, Flight Sergeant Rimmer's flying log book being endorsed, 'Disobedience of orders'; rather more than a slapped wrist, but one that allowed him to carry on and complete his training.

Hollingworth roll-down area

At the Hollingworth Hall site the recovery crew jacked the aircraft up, lowered the undercarriage, then rolled the machine down to the trees where the wings were detached prior to the whole assembly being taken off by road. The aircraft was soon returned to service. And after a short leave most crew members too were back in the air. Not the concussed Sergeant Mance, however, for he was medically screened from further flying duties. Flight Sergeant 'Ted' Rimmer, for his part, went on to fly Wellingtons operationally, surviving the war, and finally leaving the Service as a warrant officer in 1946.

In 1992, however, in company with author Mr David W. Earl, and aviation artist and crash-site researcher Mr Alan Jones, Mr Rimmer returned to the area. He was able to point out the route taken as the Anson was rolled down to the road, but he had to confess that, as he had come to earth on a dark and misty pre-dawn, he was unable to say exactly whereabouts on the moor he had done so.

Fortunately, the same did not apply to researcher Mr Alan Jones, for he remembered just where the aircraft had come into view as he had ascended Cow Lane on his initial visit as a schoolboy back in 1944; although, recalling that visit he discovered himself to be still chagrined at having been forced to stand at the barrier a hundred yards off, whereas a boy who had arrived just a little earlier had been permitted to climb into the cockpit. Another witness able to re-locate the site – conceivably that same to-be-envied boy – was Mr Arnold Willerton, of Hyde, who as a lad had cycled from home to view the aircraft the morning after it had put down and remembered with great clarity the maps, headsets, and other flight paraphernalia still strewn around the cockpit.

Both these remembrances notwithstanding, in 2012 the slope on Hollingworth Hall Moor produced no tangible evidence of this forcible – rather than forced – landing. But that was hardly to be wondered at considering the lapse of time; particularly as the machine was barely damaged and the site so easily accessible for the recovery team.

VISITING THE SITE

The Hobson Moor Road leaves the A6018 Stalybridge-Mottram Road at Roe Cross (SJ 98623 96570). Having followed the moor road, convenient parking will be found between Landslow Green Farm and Hall Farm. The gate through which the aircraft was recovered is at SK 00070 97635, the crash site lying 340 yards up the moor on a heading of 308°M.

5. Bristol Blenheim Mk.4 T1884
Harrop Edge, south-east of Stalybridge

SJ 98118 96494 259 m

Unit and Squadron: No. 105 Squadron, RAF Swanton Morley
(East Dereham, Norfolk), No. 2 Group, Bomber Command

Date: 28 November 1940

Crew: three, baled out successfully:

* Sergeant E.A. Costello-Bowan, pilot
* Sergeant Broom, navigator
* Sergeant Cameron, wireless operator/air gunner

When the more powerfully-engined Mk.4 Blenheim took over the operational task from the obsolescent Mk.1, No.105 Squadron was among the seventy squadrons which would eventually be equipped with the new version, receiving its first Mk.4 on 28 June 1940 although, at that time, nobody on the squadron was qualified to fly it. Indeed, it was not until early July that squadron pilots could be checked out on the type. Six months later, however, on 28 November 1940, with that mortifyingly too-early delivery well behind them, No.105 Squadron was to encounter a hiatus of a different sort.

On that November night, during a particularly foggy period, the squadron's fighter-bombers, among them Sergeant Costello-Bowan's T1884, raided Cologne, bombing the city, and strafing on opportunity during the return flight. While they were away, however, the fog had thickened over the United Kingdom, and particularly over their base at Swanton Morley, just north of East Dereham, in Norfolk.

Target, Cologne

In such conditions just one of the returning raiders managed to scrape into Swanton Morley. Another actually overflew the airfield, but then crashed. The crew of Blenheim T1884, lost above cloud, but expecting to be in the vicinity of their Norfolk base, finally fixed themselves over Liverpool! Nonplussed, Sergeant Costello-Bowan turned inland, and at 0100 hours, with the fuel very low, ordered his crew to bale out. The navigator and wireless operator/air gunner landed near Ashton-under-Lyne, and Sergeant Costello-Bowan himself, near Stalybridge. Left to its own devices the aircraft flew on, twice menacing Wrigleyfold Farm in its circling descent before crashing into Harrop Edge, just beyond the farm, and burning out.

Being close to roads, and on working farmland, the site was cleared within a matter of days, ostensibly by the RAF, but arguably just as much by such scavenging children as the enterprising young souvenir-hunter, Arnold Willerton, of Hyde, who visited the crash scene on his bicycle. What other debris may have been left behind on this pasture had, by 2010, long since been ploughed under; consequently there was nothing to be seen. Despite the lapse of years, however, both Mr Willerton and Mr Ellis Summerscale, who had farmed the area all his life, were able to indicate the impact point, following which metal-detector searches turned up items that positively identified the crash site as that of a Blenheim.

The crash site, 2011

Looking towards Wrigleyfold Farm, debris scraps, 2011

VISITING THE SITE

Matley Lane leaves the A6018 Stalybridge-Mottram Road at Roe Cross (SJ 98439 96628). Soon after the junction there is restricted lay-by parking at SJ 98198 96648 virtually opposite a footpath which, within yards, passes the gate to the field where the crash occurred. The impact site lies 155 yards from the gate on a heading of 217°M, just beyond a pylon.

6. De Havilland DH60M Moth G-AAJX
Pott House Farm, Matley, Hyde

SJ 97115 96815 183 m
Operator: National Flying Services, Hanworth, Middlesex
Date: 14 May 1931
Crew: pilot, slightly injured:

• Mr Bruce Bryne Bossum, bruises and abrasions.

At 1100 hours on Thursday, 14 May 1931, owner-pilot Mr Bruce Bossum departed from the London Air Park, Hanworth – a notable early-aviation venue –, on what he later termed 'an important errand'. He expected to arrive in Blackpool, some two hundred miles off, by 1500 hours, after which he planned to return to London. Encountering adverse winds on the outbound flight, however, he ran short of fuel, and having examined a number of possible landing sites in the Matley area, chose to put down to the rear of the Rising Moon public house on Matley Lane, some twenty-five miles east of his planned track. Having refuelled he got airborne once again, but while making a clearly too-ambitious early turn onto course, was struck by a gust and crashed in a field at the adjacent Pott House Farm. After he had scrambled free, his biplane Moth, G-AAJX, was destroyed by fire.

Although not formally investigated by the Air Accident Investigation Branch (AAIB) the accident is recorded, they advise, in their 'original handwritten crash-ledger book'. It was reported, though, by the *North Cheshire Herald* on Friday, 15 May 1931, as having occurred in 'the lonely uplands of Matley'. The newspaper's account, unearthed in 2007 by Mr Bill Johnson, of Mottram, describes how Mr Bossum, 'an independent gentleman in his twenties who makes flying his hobby,' had circled Matley seven or so times before 'planing down' in the field behind the Rising Moon Inn; after which a Newton man, Mr W. Berry, had procured a supply of petrol.

Witness Mr Geoff Stevens of Stalybridge told the paper, 'He had plenty of field space to take off when he had filled up with petrol. He rose well, and was clear of the wall. He turned round at an altitude of forty feet, and I thought he would get away all right. Suddenly a strong wind swept across from the west and seemed to get the machine straight, and this caused it to come down nose first. The undercarriage struck the embankment in Mr Ollerenshaw's field and the wheels were torn off and thrown into the field. The machine turned on its side and bumped like a tank for forty yards before it stopped. The pilot tumbled out head first [as it caught fire].'

The crash scene, **North Cheshire Herald**

The Stalybridge police, it is recorded, were soon on the spot 'with the emergency van', but the aircraft had burnt out within five minutes, only the 'steel frame, the engine, and the aluminium wings' being identifiable, the heat, bystanders reported, being so intense that it could be felt on the road, forty yards away. Mr Bossum, though 'badly shocked and bleeding from nose and mouth, was able to walk to the Inn' where Mrs Rowland Firth, the wife of the licensee, made him comfortable. Later the pilot-owner walked back to survey what was left of his Moth, 'viewing the remains with a sad expression as one would who has lost a valued possession.' 'There goes five hundred nickers (£500),' he mourned. He was further quoted as saying, 'It was pretty thrilling. I was not strapped in, and this is the first time in several years flying experience that I have not been strapped. If I had been

I could not have released myself in time, owing to the awkward position of the machine after the crash.'

Layman-witness Mr Berry was somewhat mystified, noting that, having successfully taken off, 'the course he [Mr Bossum] took was the opposite direction to the north-westerly route for Blackpool'. But then an easterly turn would have been politic, with Hough Hill looming and downdrafts to be expected. Additionally a continued right-hand climbing turn would have brought the machine back over the Rising Moon and so facilitated setting course from a known position; a workmanlike practice.

Having settled somewhat, Mr Bossum was motored to Woodford and duly completed the journey to Blackpool.

Regarding the location, the newspaper has the crash occurring at Hough Hill Farm. Local knowledge, however, confirmed that 'Mr Ollerenshaw's field' (and its proximity to the road) locates the crash site at Pott House Farm, formerly separated from the Inn by just two cottages which subsequently became a single house. Regarding the departure airport (Hanworth), the paper initially talks of London, but then introduces Croydon; understandably, as that was the best known of the London airports.

The impact area, looking towards the Rising Moon

VISITING THE SITE

Matley Lane leaves the A6018 Stalybridge-Mottram Road at Roe Cross (SJ 98439 96628). Permissive parking can then be obtained at the Rising Moon Pub (SJ 96973 96672), the crash having occurred in the field to the north-east of the neighbouring Pott House Farm. The site is within walking distance of the Harrop Edge site (see immediately above) and the Matley Hall site (see immediately below).

7. De Havilland DH82A Tiger Moths
Lower Matley Hall, Matley

SJ 96918 96017 181 m
Unit and Squadron: RAF Llandow, South Wales
Date: 1 November 1946
Crew: two pilots, both uninjured

The set down site at Lower Matley Hall, 2011

Two Tiger Moths routing from Llandow (near Bridgend, South Wales) to Burnaston (Derby) became lost and short of fuel. Having circled the Shaw Hall area, some 45 miles off their planned track, they put down just before dusk in a 12-acre field at Lower Matley Hall, overlooking Victoria Street, Matley. Though neither aircraft was damaged the field was unsuited to a take off and they had to be dismantled and shipped away by road.

Mr Alan Jones, of Stalybridge, supplied a newsreport of the incident while Mr Ian Wynne, of Castle Farm, actually remembered where they set down. The long-time owners of the property, Mr and Mrs Margaret and Andrew Wager, had no recollection of the event. Nor could Hendon RAF Museum locate an incident report.

VISITING THE SITE

Permissive parking may be obtained at the Rising Moon Pub (SJ 96973 96672). A footpath across the road from the pub leads south-eastwards and soon enters a well-worth-seeing wooded gorge. If the footpath is left to its own devices as it emerges from the wood at SJ 97154 96261, then the site of the setdown – merely an open space, as might be expected – is 370 yards off on a heading of 220°M.

Dovestone Reservoir Area

8. Gloster Gamecock J7920
Diglea Farm, Diggle

SE 01192 08351 239 m

Unit and Station: No. 43 Squadron, RAF Tangmere

Date: 19 May 1927

Pilot: unhurt:

- Flying Officer Bertram William Trelawney Hare

Gloster Gamecock

In the course of a detached duty from their home station of RAF Tangmere, near Chichester, four Gloster Gamecocks of No. 43 Squadron, having departed from RAF Sealand, near Chester, ran into a substantial amount of cloud as they approached the high ground at Standedge. Realising the danger of attempting to penetrate the build-up, the leader made the judicious decision to turn away. However, on preparing to signal his intentions, he discovered that one of his quartet, Flying Officer Bertram Hare, was no longer keeping station. He took what was now his trio into the turn, but once on a safe heading, directed the others to support him in an area search. Watchers saw the three aircraft circle for some time, only it was clear that they found no sign of their colleague, for eventually they were seen to close into a 'Vee', and pass out of sight into the mist.

As it transpired, and as people in Diggle, just to the south of the highest ground, were already aware, Flying Officer Hare, presumably having suffered some engine malfunction, had found it necessary to set his machine down. The field he chose was a large pasture at Diglea Farm, on Boat Lane, just to the north-east of the Diggle Hotel. By mischance he undershot his approach and clipped the top of a drystone wall with his propeller, the impact flipping the machine over, leaving Flying Officer Hare suspended in his inverted cockpit. There was no fire, however, and the aviator was soon pulled clear having suffered little more than a good shaking.

The press report

The local newspaper, in covering the event in its next edition, dated 28 May 1927, noted, 'The aeroplane which collided with Diggle Hill is the first on record to be brought down in Saddleworth.' It then went on, 'It appears that one of the fleet of aeroplanes which passed through Saddleworth recently came in contact with Diggle Hill and was brought down and when it reached the ground completely turned over. The pilot fortunately was uninjured. There was fog at the time of the accident.'

Mr Jack Taylor, of Diglea, witness

In September 2005 Mr Jack Taylor, of Diglea, was the only person encountered who knew anything of the incident, although to collect his thoughts he went even further back to a world that had already been radically changed by 1927. 'I was born in Petrograd,' he smiled, 'where my father was installing textile looms for the Russians. But just after I was born, in 1915, with the Russian Revolution boiling up, he had to send my mother and us three children home, not leaving himself until after the trouble had erupted.' He pointed outside. 'Regarding the plane – a Gamecock, it was said – it put down in what they called the Cricket Field, although its real name is Broad Meadow. It's rough now, but it was smooth enough back then, for the Wriggly Mill School played on it; although I only actually saw one match. On the day of the crash, though, a great crowd gathered around at the wall where the plane had finished up. Then they cleared it away.'

The Cricket Field, with Boat Lane as its left-hand boundary

Little enough, but gratifying in the extreme, sufficing, as it did, to confirm just where this relatively minor upset had occurred. Concurring with Mr Taylor, the local newspaper commented that 'hundreds of sightseers visited the scene of the accident during the evening', recording too that Flying Officer Hare had been accommodated for the night by a Mr Marsden of Dobcross, a mile or so south-west of Diggle.

By early 2013 no RAF accident report had been found regarding this incident, and nothing related to the upset was visible at the site; although by then Boat Lane had long become that section of the walkers' Standedge Trail paralleling the southern end of the Standedge rail and canal tunnels. Yet if nothing came to light regarding the technical reason which forced Flying Officer Hare to make a landing, rather than continue to hold his place with the formation; and while nothing was known of the findings of the inquiry; records do exist of Flying Officer Hare's subsequent career.

Air historian Mr Malcolm Barrass, having referred to contemporary Air Force Lists, established that Flying Officer Hare had joined No. 43 Squadron on 1 July 1925, subsequently becoming their pilotage [navigation] officer. He had remained with them until 30 September 1927, when he had been posted to No. 11 Squadron, being promoted to flight lieutenant on 1 January 1928.

In attempting to determine which of No. 43 Squadron's Gamecocks was involved, records showed that of those on the establishment both J7920 and J7904 left the squadron in 1927 'after being damaged'; both subsequently re-appearing with other units. As J7920 left in May, and the setdown occurred on 19 May, this would seem to be the particular Gamecock in question.

For completeness, and for posterity, it should be recorded that Ranger Phillip Shaw, of Glossop, supplied an enthusiast source which held that the date was 28 March 1927. This was disproved by the date of the newspaper account. But it was also held that the aircraft was an Avro 504K, of No. 5 Flying Training School, RAF Sealand; the aerodrome from which the flight had been operating on that leg of its progress. A parallel search of Avro 504K accident reports, however, proved as fruitless as that for the Gamecock, so that positive determination will have to await future archival research.

VISITING THE SITE

Both permissive and opportunity parking can be found near the Diggle Hotel at SE 00887 08042. A track then leads north-east to join the Standedge-cum-Oldham Trail. After 470 yards (at SE 01183 08356) the track passes abeam the set-down site, 120 yards into the fields on a heading of 130°M.

Wessington Head Moor

9. Junkers Ju88-A5 (B3DC)
Dean Head Hill, north-west of Black Hill

SE 06602 05737 516 m

Service and Unit: Luftwaffe *Kampfgeschwader 54*, Lille, France

Date: 15 April 1941

Crew: three survived, initially attempted to evade capture.

On the night of 15 April 1941, Junkers Ju88 (B3DC) of No. 54 '*Totenkopf*' (Death's Head) *Kampfgeschwader* (bomber group), based at Lille, in France, was shot down by an anti-aircraft battery at Almonbury, Huddersfield, and crashed at Dean Head Hill, on Wessenden Head Moor, to the north-west of Black Hill. The aircraft 'fell within a mile of the Isle of Skye Inn', which stood at the junction of the A635 and Wessenden Head Road (at SE 07709 07239) but has long been demolished, although its foundation terrace survives. Later, three German aircrew were discovered hiding in the area and initially taken to the Inn.

The crash site is within yards of the (partially staked) footpath running north-west from Black Hill to meet the A635. It was searched by enthusiast groups in the seventies, but whether any debris was found is not known. Certainly no aircraft-derived material was discovered in the course of metal-detector searches up to early 2013.

Welcome additional input was supplied by aviation author Mr David W. Earl. Having noted that the above information conforms, in the main, with a feature article in the *Huddersfield Daily Examiner* dated 12 May 1979, he advised that an 'After the Battle' publication, *The Blitz: Then and Now*, holds that the Ju88 bearing the registration B3DC actually crashed at Rughouse Farm, Holcombe Burnell, in Devon; which means that a caveat has to be added, not regarding the Dean-Head Hill site itself, but the specific Ju88 involved.

The Dean Head crash site

VISITING THE SITE

Adequate parking is available by the A635 at SE 05081 06303. From there the south-easterly footpath crossing Dean Head Moss passes abeam the crash site after 0.99 miles (1.6 km). An alternative, although less satisfactory, parking spot is the minimal lay-by at SE 05601 06423. From there the way is off-path initially but having joined the main-route it arrives abeam the site after 0.75 miles (1.2 km). Once abeam, the site is 100 yards off to the north-east.

10. Junkers Ju88
Tooleyshaw Moss, south-west of Black Hill

SE 06692 03800 493 m
Service: Luftwaffe
Date: c.1941

This crash site, long attributed to a Junkers Ju88, is to the south-west of Black Hill, on Tooleyshaw Moss, and only yards from the now-paved Pennine Way. In the 1980s Mr Kevin Wynn, of Knottingley, introducing researcher Mr John Ownsworth to the site, remembered debris being scattered there. He also remembered, however, that several groups had busied themselves in various digs during the seventies. Mr Ownsworth found nothing on that occasion, nor was there any result from metal-detector scans as late as early 2013.

Holme Moss TV mast

The Tooleyshaw Moss site

VISITING THE SITE

The route to this site is detailed in Main Section 16, Sliddens Moor, above. Nothing whatsoever to be seen, but it may well provide the excuse for a breath-catching pause between Crowden and Black Hill.

Holmfirth Area

11. Miles Master Mk.3 W8506
Hepworth, near the Victoria Inn

SE 17999 05289 339 m, touchdown
SE 18054 05305 339 m, terminal run onto rough ground
Unit and Station: No. 16 (Polish) Service Flying Training School,
RAF Newton (Nottingham), No. 21 Group, Flying Training Command
Date: 21 March 1943
Pilot: solo, injured:

- Pupil Pilot Leading Aircraftman Henryk Kowalski, Polish Air Force under British Command

On 21 March 1943 Polish trainee pilot Leading Aircraftman Henryk Kowalski, an advanced pupil with just under two hundred hours of flying experience, was briefed for what appears to have been a pupil-led solo formation detail from RAF Newton. The formation duly got airborne at 1535 hours but encountered low-visibility conditions in which Leading Aircraftman Kowalski was unable to hold station. Seeing the other aircraft disappear into the mist, and now cast upon his own resources, he found that he had no idea where the leader had brought them. Though hopelessly lost he continued to search about, until, having been airborne for just over two hours and with fuel running short, he decided to put the aircraft down. Accordingly, at 1740 hours, he made a forced-landing in a field adjacent to, and to the rear of, the Victoria Inn at Hepworth, Yorkshire, some fifty miles, as it transpired, from his base.

The landing run did not go well, and Leading Aircraftman Kowalski was injured when the aircraft tipped up on rough ground, although to what degree is not recorded. The aircraft, however, was so badly damaged that it had to be written off.

The subsequent enquiry concentrated upon the command and control of the formation, the squadron commander rather lamely submitting that in future only instructors should lead formations when the weather was in any doubt, leaving RAF Newton's officer commanding to note tersely, 'I agree.'

Mr Phillip Tinker, Spring Head Farm, Upper Cumberworth

Mr Phillip Tinker, of Spring Head Farm, Upper Cumberworth, not only recalled the incident but was able to indicate the landing site. 'I saw it from where I was working,' he explained. 'The Master came curving in, then ran the length of the field, but ended by tipping nose down and tail up. I don't know what state the pilot was in, or what happened to him then. But the RAF soon arrived and took over, only they couldn't repair the plane, so next day Leslie Alsop pulled it out to the road using his Fordson and it was loaded onto a Queen Mary and driven off.'

Even in early 2011 the field Leading Aircraftman Kowalski selected still seemed estimable for the purpose, so it could be that he simply came in a few knots too fast, or touched down a little too far into the field. As is so often the case when searching constantly worked farmland, and particularly as the incident was so trifling, a metal detector search found no evidence.

The terminal site, with the Victoria Inn behind the trees

VISITING THE SITE

Parking is to be found beside the A616 at SE 17935 05253, after which it is a 100 yard walk across the field to the site.

12. Airspeed Oxford Mk.2 AB662
Gatefoot Farm, New Mill, Shepley

SE 18221 08521 285 m, impact with barn

SE 18175 08395 300 m, debris spread

Unit and Station: No. 14 (Pilots) Advanced Flying Unit, RAF Ossington (near Newark, Nottinghamshire), No. 2 Group,

Flying Training Command

Date: 14 April 1942

Pilot: solo pupil pilot, killed:

- Sergeant Melvin Harry Smith, Royal Canadian Air Force

In the early hours of 14 April 1942 Sergeant Melvin Smith, an American from Illinois, serving with the Royal Canadian Air Force, was dispatched from RAF Ossington, near Newark, to carry out solo night circuits and landings. It would have been normal enough to temporarily clear from the circuit in order to practise homing to the airfield and rejoining the landing pattern, but the time came when Sergeant Smith lost sight of the flare path altogether and realised that he no longer knew where the airfield was. This was not that surprising, for the flare path, the sole lighting showing in the blackout, was formed by nothing more than two faltering lines of paraffin-fuelled gooseneck flares; the burners employed, moreover, being hooded, and fully visible only from the approach direction.

Sergeant Smith might have been expected to relocate himself using contingency procedures which would have been demonstrated to him on previous sorties. As it was, he strayed some forty-six miles from low-lying Ossington, and at 0500 hours crashed into a barn on a 1,000-feet-above-sea-level hillside at New Mill, near Holmfirth. The aircraft disintegrated on impact, killing Sergeant Smith outright.

The former barn, Gatefoot Farm

Mrs Catherine Wilson, of Gatefoot Lane, readily recalled the day of the crash, although she had always thought the aircraft was a much lighter trainer. 'It had crashed along the barn just across from us,' she recalled, 'but we weren't allowed to go over there until it had been cleared away. Fortunately it hit the barn, rather than the house, so nobody in the farm was hurt.'

Mr Frank Brook, former resident of Gatewood Farm

Mr Frank Brook, in 2005 of New Mill, but formerly resident in Gatefoot Farm, had even less difficulty in recalling the shock of the aircraft's arrival; and he had no doubts about its type. 'It was an Oxford,' he said, 'and it came from the Shepley direction and crashed into the gable end of the barn. It took off the roof, then scraped along one wall, but just missed where our family was, in the house at the end. One of the big radial engines finished up beside the house, but the other rolled downhill to the Junction Pub – it's now The Crossroads. The rest of the wreckage had broken down the drystone walls bordering the road and finished up in the field beyond. In fact, that's where we found the pilot's body: he was Canadian Air Force.'

Mrs Catherine Wilson, facing the barn, has her back to the terminal site

He paused, considering. 'Before that, I remember Dad calling through the dark for a match because all the electrics had gone. Until my sister pointed out that the whole place reeked of petrol.' He grinned. 'And I remember one of the local men, a Home Guard, arriving, and although we'd been wandering about all over, ordering, "All *civilians* out of the field." Then the army came from Shepley, and in the end the RAF took away the wreckage in their Queen Marys. Fortunately there was no fire, and the house was untouched. Then, too, a great stone from the barn had fallen down and landed between two cows, but without touching either. And we got compensation for rebuilding. In fact, original stones from the barn were used to make the coping stones on the boundary wall.'

Material from the barn, re-used as coping stones

VISITING THE SITE

Gatefoot Farm and its barn have long become private residences and show no signs of the fatal crash of 1943. On the roadside drystone wall in line with the barn, however, the coping stones originating from the damaged barn, mute though they are, still tell the tale.

13. De Havilland DH82A Tiger Moth
Spring Head Farm, Upper Cumberworth, near Hepworth

SE 17932 07099 372 m, touchdown, on the ridge's brow
SE 17937 07139 377 m, terminal site, the drystone wall
Unit and Station: Flying Training Command
Date: 1940-41
Occupant: solo, unidentified pilot, uninjured

In the early wartime years a Tiger Moth, presumably lost or short of fuel, made a forced-landing approach to a field high on the ridge just across the road from Spring Head Farm, Upper Cumberworth. Mr Phillip Tinker was able to describe how the incident had struck him.

'The pilot must have seen how the field flattened towards the top of the ridge, only misjudged the gradient lower down. So, at the last moment, although he throttled up and lifted his nose, the slope out-climbed him. The Tiger Moth ran on and into the drystone wall and although the propeller splintered, it carved a great gap before the engine stopped. The pilot, however, wasn't hurt, so Harry Needham, the local ARP warden, took him off and fed him tea until the RAF came for him. As for the aeroplane, that wasn't much use, and it was soon pulled down to the road and taken off by Queen Mary trailer.' Mr Tinker paused. 'Strangely, in the late 1990s a glider came down in the identical spot. It had been flying from Hull to Great Hucklow, and chose to put down there. Again, nobody was hurt.'

Mr Tinker maintained that the repair in the wall, necessitated after the Tiger Moth's propeller had chewed its way through, was still evident, but not even this memento of the crash was to be discerned by this particular townie's gaze.

Although archive sources failed to provide a match, future research might be aided by Mr Tinker's assertion that the aircraft was in camouflage drab rather than Flying Training Command yellow.

Mr Phillip Tinker indicates the crash site

The terminal site, looking down towards Spring Head Farm

VISITING THE SITE

Roadside parking can be found near Spring Head Farm on Windmill Lane, east of the crossroads with Dick Edge Lane. The crash site is upslope to the north of the road.

North-East of the Area

14. Wellington Mk.4 Z1327, Farnley Bank
Farnley Tyas, south-east of Huddersfield

SE 16542 13643 164 m, cottage impact
SE 16627 13355 221 m, terminal extent of the wreckage spray
Unit and Station: No. 460 Squadron, Royal Australian Air Force,
RAF Breighton (Selby, Yorkshire), No. 1 Group, Bomber Command
Date: 17 February 1942
Crew: six, all killed:

- Sergeant James Henry Ware, RAAF, screen pilot
- Sergeant Robert Litchfield Tresidder, RAAF, pilot
- Sergeant William Leonard Ashplant, RAF Volunteer Reserve, observer (navigator)
- Sergeant Frederick Dutton, RAFVR, screen wireless operator/air gunner
- Sergeant Cyril Caradoe Davies, RAFVR, wireless operator
- Sergeant Cyril Raymond Dickeson, RAFVR, air gunner

In November 1941 Wellington-equipped No. 460 Squadron of the Royal Australian Air Force came into being at RAF Breighton, near Selby, in Yorkshire, and by February 1942 was nearing operational readiness. It was always to be a multi-national squadron, although predominantly Australian, so that, on 17 February 1942, when Wellington Z1327 crashed, its crew contained both RAAF and RAF personnel.

Sergeant James Ware and the crew of Z1327 had been carrying out a night-navigational exercise that had initially taken them south and south-west to Peterborough, Harwell and Pershore. They had then been required to head eastwards to Sywell, near Northampton, before steering a northerly course for Breighton, the short, easterly leg to Sywell being designed to keep them clear of the Midland's high moors. In any circumstances it would have been a fair test of their capability as a crew, particularly as many would have been trained in uncluttered, brightly-lit Commonwealth lands rather than totally blacked-out England. On this occasion, however, they had to contend with a typical February weather pattern as well, giving extensive cloud over all high ground, and with snow dramatically reducing visibility; indeed, neighbouring RAF Snaith, another Bomber Command unit, had cancelled its own night-flying programme outright.

The direction-finding facility at the controlling RAF Holme-on-Spalding-Moor, of which RAF Breighton was a satellite, would record that the two wireless operators on board the Wellington had obtained bearings and fixes during the flight. It was evident, however, that the observer – the navigator – Sergeant William Ashplant, had not made adequate use of these, for when the aircraft crashed it was found to be thirty-eight miles to the west of its planned track.

The first indication the residents of Farnley Tyas had of the impending disaster was when they heard an aircraft circling overhead. Mrs Janet Sykes, of Farnley Bank, recalled the singular experience of her father-in-law, Mr Harry Sykes.

'Having walked Laura, his wife, to her nursing shift up in Farnley Tyas, Harry was returning to Low Common Farm on the field path. He'd been aware of this aircraft circling and getting lower, although a thick mist had confused him about its height and direction. But he'd left Farnley Bank Wood and was approaching the wall where the footpath crosses the Woodsome Road when he heard the engines cut. The next thing he knew was that he

was actually in the road, physically unhurt having regained consciousness, but being tended by two policemen. What had happened was that the plane had hit a cottage down the hill, skipped the road, missed him by feet, and exploded in flames on the slope behind him, the blast throwing him clean across the wall.'

Mr Harry Sykes, thrown clean across the wall

Mr J.R. Winn, in 2005 resident in Longwood, but a youth of sixteen in 1942, would be quoted in the *Huddersfield Examiner* of 19 February 1979 as remembering his mother exclaiming, 'The woods are all on fire!' The article then related that he had run towards Farnley Bank Wood, to find that the aircraft had demolished the roof and an eaves wall of a cottage; that it had then crossed the Woodsome Road 'shedding its wings and engines, spreading wreckage in its trail and up to thirty yards up the hillside and spraying the area ahead with burning petrol.' Mr Winn's account also described how the wreckage was eventually taken away by Queen Mary trailers.

The RAF accident-report summary does not mention the cottage, merely recording that the aircraft 'flew into trees on rising ground in poor visibility, killing all on board.' But the fundamental cause of the accident was all too clear: the aircraft had been descended blind through cloud. However, that the crew should have positively established themselves over Northampton's Sywell airfield and then drifted as far as thirty-eight miles to the west in just one hundred northerly miles seems unlikely. Such a gross westerly error would be fully explained, however, if they had mistaken, say, Banbury for Northampton, and turned northwards too early; for additionally this would explain why they were twenty miles short on their planned along-track distance for the Breighton overhead – albeit just a few minutes' flying time – when they chose to spiral down to break cloud.

On board, as all available eyes stared down to make out Breighton's flare path, the atmosphere would have been one of relief to be finishing the long flight mixed with tense anticipation; but certainly not with apprehension, for nobody would have doubted that they were in the vicinity of twenty-four-feet-above-sea-level Breighton. And so they would have persisted in their descent, well aware that the cloud base was very low, but expecting to see the lights at any moment; and more especially as their altimeter reading neared five hundred feet. It was their tragic misfortune, of course, that, having descended too early, and so far to the left of track, they had spiralled below the cloud-shrouded, near-1,000-feet-above-sea-level Castle Hill and were steering into some adjacent high ground when their left wing struck the 537-feet-above-sea-level cottage. The stricken machine then impacted into the slope beyond and burst into flames, the crew almost certainly dying unaware of what had happened. Providentially, both Mr Clifford Hardy, the resident of the cottage, and an elderly lady living next door were unscathed.

Looking back along the line of flight, across the Woodsome Road, towards the cottage

Looking ahead along the line of flight, over the Woodsome Road, towards the terminal area, just short of Farnley Bank Wood

At the time, the loss of their six crew members and a Wellington would have been a daunting blow to both the air and groundcrews of the newly formed

No. 460 Squadron. But this was just the precursor. For in the course of their early operational flying they were to lose twenty Wellingtons, together with nearly all their crews, in a period of just three months. Indeed, before the cessation of hostilities, with 6,264 operational sorties behind them, having re-equipped with Lancasters, and with a regular establishment of just 200 aircrew, the squadron was to suffer 1,018 aircrew deaths (589 Australian) and to lose 188 heavy bombers.

The loss of this particular aircraft and crew is commemorated in a memorial centre in Australia's Ayers Rock by a 1995 photograph of the 2006 owner, Mrs Marjorie Russell, indicating the truncated cottage end where the necessarily-demolished No.3 Farnley Bank had been.

Mrs Marjorie Russell in 1995, indicating where No.3 Farnley Bank stood

In 2013, although traces of the erstwhile No.3 were still to be seen in the stonework of the extensively refurbished No. 4 Farnley Bank, there was no other surface evidence of the tragedy.

Mrs Marjory Russell pointing to traces of No. 3

VISITING THE SITE

Parking is not recommended on the narrow Woodsome Road in the vicinity of the terminal impact site. A safer area is found by turning off onto the Farnley Bank Road at SE 16853 13898. From the area given as the initial impact point, the footpath used by Mr Sykes crosses the Woodsome Road to the terminal point.

15. Armstrong Whitworth Whitley
Emley Moor, south-east of Huddersfield

SE 22898 13890 224 m

Unit and Station: RAF Bomber Command

Date: c.1941

Crew: presently unidentified: uninjured

Armstrong Whitworth Whitley

Enthusiast lists and local lore have it that in or about 1941 a Whitley crashed on Emley Moor – long since the site of the region's television mast. Investigations, however, showed that the machine did not crash but made a successful precautionary landing in a field at Crawshaw Farm. The aircraft remained on the ground for some days, but after a section of drystone wall had been removed, and a swathe had been cut through unripe, but standing corn, it was flown off once more.

Retired builder Mr Ken Matley, of Thorncliff Green, had vivid memories of the event. 'At the time,' he said, 'I'd have been 23, or so, and lived at Cross Roads. At about seven in the morning we heard this aircraft pass low overhead, and realised that it had come down nearby. On the way to work, therefore, I stopped my motorbike to have a look, but I didn't have the time to wait long: being late would've meant risking the sack. I've no idea what type it was, except that it was a bomber. Although it had dropped all its bombs, for there were none on board. The crew were bunched about Major Wright, of Crawshaw Farm – it was his land – and as far as I know, he took them in until the RAF came for them.

The plane was there for some days, maybe even a week, with the army guarding it, for it drew lots of people. Then it was refuelled, from cans, I remember, and on the Sunday – therefore there were crowds free to watch – it took off to the north, towards Grange Moor, running through a gap in the wall and a pathway cut through the unripe corn. It seemed to only scrape over the road, which was worrying, for the ground drops very steeply away beyond that. But it got clear in the end.'

No more details of this forced-landing have yet come to hand, and whether or not this was, indeed, one of the few bombers to come to earth in the Peakland area in the course of operations, is not known.

Mr Matley's account is certainly borne out by the location, and particularly by the fact that standing corn had to be cut, and a section of drystone wall dismantled, in order to facilitate the take-off. As a type the Whitley was customarily operated from grass airfields, but this area, though flat enough, and spacious enough with the wall opened up, was an unprepared surface, and the corn, had it not been cut, would have created a prohibitive amount of drag. As it was, the take-off – with the aircraft evidently being held down in order to more rapidly gain adequate flying speed – was as successful as the set-down, for all that the take-off run appeared fraught to the apprehensive onlookers.

As Mr Matley pointed out, nowadays the site has little enough in common with the way it was in 1941. 'There were only a few houses then,' he recalled, 'and no trees and bushes. But since then they've taken coal from the place, and even at the time there was a pond and a tip nearby, both of which the pilot missed.' Mr Matley pointed to the two fields in question, separated once again by a drystone wall – somewhat ruinous at this remove of years – but both smooth-ploughed, observing, 'They weren't smooth like that then, but rough.'

Not a crash at all then, but of possible interest to the walker traversing this moorland area. A traverse to be made, perhaps, a little gingerly, in reflective awareness that a previous TV aerial, equally towering, was brought to earth by an asymmetric load of ice …

VISITING THE SITE

Roadside parking is available beside Common Lane at SE 22779 13951. A field path then leads to the terminal area of the set-down site, 150 yards away on a heading of 121°M.

Penistone Area

16. Fairey Battle, Penistone Viaduct

SE 25287 04013 225 m

Unit and Station: No. 300 Squadron,
Polish Air Force under British Command, RAF Bramcote, Nuneaton,
No. 6 (Training) Group, Bomber Command
Date: *c.*1940
Occupants: unidentified: two, Polish Air Force under British Command,
uninjured

The Fairey Battle

Between July and August 1940, four Polish Fairey Battle light-bomber
squadrons – Nos.300 to 304 – were raised at RAF Bramcote, in Warwickshire.
The crews were initially converted onto Battles by a cadre of Poles trained at
RAF Hucknall, in Nottinghamshire, but by November 1940, with the type
having proved so disastrous on operations, all four squadrons had been
re-equipped with Wellingtons. Before that, however, one of the Battles was
destroyed in making a forced-landing to the north-east of Penistone. The
aircraft struck a kinked, drystone wall – still shown on the 2002 edition of
the 1:25,000 Ordnance Survey map – and had to be written off, although
the occupants were uninjured.

In the 1980s the incumbents of two immediately-adjacent farms, High
Lee and High Lea [*sic*, Lee and Lea!], described the occurrence to researcher

Mr John Ownsworth. Little more could be determined, however – Polish MOD archives were, unusually, unable to help –, and even the drystone wall in question had been demolished, leaving a single spacious field. Prior to the demolition, the wall ran uphill from SE 14100 03890 208 m, via SE 24150 03950, thence to the reference given.

The Penistone Viaduct site

VISITING THE SITE

Any convenient lay-by off the A628, as at SE 25440 04161, gives access to the fields in which the Battle came down. From that lay-by the site is just 250 yards distant on a heading of 216°M.

17. Trainer, Elementary Flying Training School type
Bella Vista Farm, Penistone

SE 22770 01874 339 m
Unit and Station: Flying Training Command
Date: 1939-45
Occupant(s): unidentified, uninjured

The Bella Vista field

An Elementary Flying Training School machine – either a Tiger Moth or a Magister – made a forced landing in a field below Bella Vista Farm, Penistone. After touching down it struck and penetrated a drystone wall, suffering damage which necessitated its recovery by road some days later. At the time the location was 'the third field below the farm', but the field pattern having changed in the interim, the reference given here relates to the upper part of the undivided field bordering the public road. No further details have become available and nobody could be found who knew anything more than hearsay.

VISITING THE SITE

Anyone wishing to visit the site, located in the second field to the right of the farm drive from the Hartcliffe Road, should apply for permission at Bella Vista.

18. De Havilland D82A Tiger Moth T5541
Wortley, Sheffield

SK 32160 98640 193 m

Unit and Station: No. 25 (Pilots) Elementary Flying Training School, RAF Hucknall, No. 21 Group, Flying Training Command

Date: 15 April 1943

Crew: solo pupil pilot, uninjured

- Leading Aircraftman Jerzy Lenartowicz, Polish Air Force under British Command.

On the afternoon of 15 April 1943, in the course of his second solo cross-country sortie, and with just six hours' solo, Pupil-Pilot Leading Aircraftman Lenartowicz became lost and at 1620 hours, after an hour and twenty minute flight, made a precautionary landing near Wortley, to the west of Sheffield. The aircraft was damaged, but being assessed as 'repairable on site' was, presumably, flown off. Leading Aircraftman Lenartowicz's squadron commander praised the pupil's selection of a forced-landing site, and his execution of the manoeuvre but categorised the incident as avoidable, the pilot having become lost. Just the same it was decided that there was no necessity for either punishment or endorsement.

Having received his wings, and his commission, Flying Officer Lenartowicz served with various anti-aircraft co-operation units before converting to fighters and joining No. 133 Wing at Coolham Advanced Landing Ground, Sussex, just before D-Day. He was discharged as a flight lieutenant on 17 December 1948 having previously been released to study at London's Northern Polytechnic.

The set-down area, Bromley, Wortley

The location given by the RAF was merely 'Mile from Wortley village', which, as noted elsewhere, was all the salvage teams needed, their aim being to determine exact cause rather than exact location; after all, once they cleared the debris, who would ever be bothered about the location … However, Farmer Tom White, of Sycamore Farm who, in 1942, had made a ring from the perspex of Hudson AM531 (see *Central Region*, page 154), and was also conversant with sundry German bombs dropped locally, indicated the area to the south-east of the village, 'Over towards Bromley, beyond the A616 and Pea Field Lane, and in those days the fields there were even bigger.'

VISITING THE SITE

Various opportunity roadside parking exists near the set-down location.

19. Dornier Do217
Penistone Agricultural Showground

SE 24800 03500
Service: Luftwaffe
Date: c.1940–42

Roy Taylor, at the showground site

Researcher Mr John Ownsworth's cousin, Mr Graham Wilson, a schoolboy during the early war years, remembers seeing this aircraft which came down on the ground traditionally used for the Penistone Agricultural Show, now long since a housing estate. He and his brother, John, remember that it had landed on the flat pastures and was standing on its undercarriage but that it had a great hole in one of its wings. They recall too, that the crew, on emerging, gave themselves up.

It might be observed here, that, in the course of researching this Peakland series, many – indeed, very many – serendipitous encounters occurred in which a person, encountered purely by chance, proved to be the one person with first-hand knowledge of the event. Researching this location, however, had a coincidental twist all of its own. Having finally penetrated the blocked-off roads of the heavily built-over location and arrived at the GPS fix supplied by Mr John Ownsworth, random passer-by Mr Roy Taylor was asked to confirm that this was indeed the former

Penistone showground site. Mr Taylor did so, but on learning that the enquiry had to do with crashed aircraft, pointed towards the far side of Penistone: 'In that case, you want to speak to my father-in-law, John Ownsworth …'

Barnsley Area

20. Gloster Gladiator K6133
Hermit House Farm, Gawber, near Barnsley

SE 31967 06999 118 m
Unit and Station: No. 72 Squadron, RAF Church Fenton,
No. 12 (Fighter) Group, Fighter Command
Date: 23 July 1937
Pilot: solo, killed:
- Acting Pilot Officer Philip Hughes Crompton

Gloster Gladiator

On 23 July 1937 Acting Pilot Officer Philip Crompton, of No. 72 Squadron, with just under 200 hours' experience, was flying one of the RAF's first-line fighters, the newly developed Gloster Gladiator, from RAF Sealand, near Chester, to RAF Church Fenton, in Yorkshire. In the course of the flight he ran into bad visibility and crashed at Hermit House Farm, Gawber, near Barnsley. Acting Pilot Officer Crompton did not survive the impact.

Witnesses reported that they had heard the aircraft circling around and flying very low. 'Almost immediately,' one would tell the coroner, 'there was a loud bang and the plane burst into flames and burnt.' Others would relate how a man in the road rushed into the field to endeavour to help but was unable to do so owing to the extreme heat; and how people from the farm rushed with buckets of water hoping to extinguish the fire, only to find their efforts unavailing as the aircraft burnt itself out.

Gladiator K6133 at Hermit Farm (**Times Past,** *Gerald Bradbury*)

Examination of the wreckage by RAF investigators showed that the aircraft had impacted at high speed, from which it was concluded that the machine had hit the ground on being dived through low cloud. Particular care was taken to stress that Acting Pilot Officer Crompton had died from multiple injuries, and not from the fire.

It also emerged that, although the Officer Commanding at RAF Church Fenton, advised of deteriorating weather, had tried to stop the flight taking off from Sealand, communications had been such that the cancellation messages did not get through in time. Wireless telegraphy (morse) links had not been available, it transpired, while telephone communication had been 'exceedingly unsatisfactory'. Indeed, it was determined that only a telegram had got through; and that far too tardily. Accordingly, much rethinking was done regarding the local signals facilities at both Church Fenton and Sealand.

The inquiry was bound to observe, however, that this failing in communications was not the prime cause of the accident, that Acting Pilot Officer Crompton should have turned back to Sealand on encountering the bad weather. In an attempt to obviate such accidents in the future, therefore, procedures were instituted to ensure that pilots would henceforth be able to obtain both actual-weather reports and route forecasts from the Church Fenton meteorological office before they took off from Sealand. It was also to be a requirement that the Officer Commanding himself would have to authorise the departure of all such flights.

As contemporary photographs show, debris was widespread, with pieces being found up to eighty yards from the point of impact. The police were swiftly on the scene and cordoned the area off, shortly after which airmen from RAF Finningley arrived. In 2013, with the field having been in continuous use, there was, of course, no visual evidence of the crash.

Mr John Butterfield

Mrs Sandra Butterfield

VISITING THE SITE

The site is in front of the house at Hermit House Farm so visiting would be at the behest of the owners.

21. Westland Lysander P9119
Festival Road, Wath Upon Dearne, near Rotherham

SE 43577 00297 58 m

Unit and Station: No. 4 Squadron, RAF Clifton (York), No. 71 Group, Army Co-operation Command

Date: 16 January 1941

Pilot: solo, uninjured:

- Pilot Officer Algernon Christopher Chaldecott, formerly Second Lieutenant, Royal Engineers (Territorial Army)

Westland Lysander

After the outbreak of war in September 1939, No. 4 Squadron, with its cantilever-winged Lysander army co-operation monoplanes, was deployed to France as part of the British Expeditionary Force. Operated as fighting machines in their own right, however, the Lysanders were totally outclassed by the enemy fighters, so that in a thirteen-day period in May 1940 the squadron lost eleven of its aircraft. [The RAF as a whole lost 118 of the 174 Lysanders sent across the Channel!] Back in England, anticipating an invasion, the squadron was set to coastal-patrol duties, so that it was not until the end of 1940, as the perceived threat receded, that they were returned to full-time army co-operation tasks and target-tug duties.

The Lysander may have been outclassed by the German first-line fighters, but among its design characteristics was a short-field landing-and-take-off capability enhanced by a sophisticated system of automatically-operating slots and variable-camber flaps: it could be airborne well within 100 yards and could land in a far shorter space. Except that to perform in that way demanded a carefully organised approach.

No. 4 Squadron's motto was *futurem videre* – to see into the future – but on 16 January 1941 it would not have needed a crystal ball to save the day for the squadron's Pilot Officer Algernon Chaldecott, just rather more attention to what he was about. Or so his commanding officer would record.

Until 7 March 1940 Pilot Officer Chaldecott had been a second lieutenant in the Royal Engineers (Territorial Army). Since transferring to the Royal Air Force, however, he had logged just over two hundred flying hours, of which just over a hundred had been on Lysanders. On the day in question, he was sent to search for an aircraft which had gone missing between Grantham and Northampton, but at some stage on the seventy-mile return flight, he ran into bad weather. Unable to re-establish his position, he finally accepted that he was lost, and with fuel running short, decided that it would be politic to make a precautionary landing. By good fortune he saw an open area immediately ahead of him, the snow-covered playing fields, as it happened, of the Wath Upon Dearne Grammar School, near Rotherham; and some thirty miles south-west of his home station.

In its entirety the space was more than adequate for landing a Lysander, but Pilot Officer Chaldecott failed to appreciate that he had elected to make his approach onto a downslope, the result being that, as he held off, feeling for the ground, so it was falling away beneath him. As a further consequence, touching down far too far into the field, he found himself facing a wall! Except that, although by that stage there was insufficient space to lift off again, he was still rolling too fast to risk applying his pneumatically-powered brakes: on his tailwheeled aircraft this would have somersaulted him. He had no option, therefore, but to rudder the machine towards a gap in the wall. Only to have a wingtip strike, first the edge of the gap, and then a tree, slewing the Lysander to a violent halt.

Shaken, Pilot Officer Chaldecott shucked off his harness, and clambered the fourteen feet down from his cockpit to the ground. Then, shocked, but otherwise unhurt, he left the lopsided Lysander where it lay and made his way towards some nearby houses with the evident aim of seeking succour, seemingly unaware of the rapidly nearing figures running towards him.

Mr Maurice Hobson, of Rawmarsh, recalled the set-down as it had appeared to him as a schoolboy back in 1941. 'We'd walked from school', he explained, 'up what is now Festival Road, but at that time was just a path past the Grammar School playing fields, and were some way along Sandygate when we heard the sound of this plane's engine. We looked back, and saw it touching down. The playing fields were the biggest space around, only they clearly weren't long enough, for the plane ran on into a paling fence, and then into a stone wall. But the pilot seemed to have headed for a gap where people had climbed it, for the plane's nose went through the gap. One wing struck the wall, though, and then a tree after that, and broke off. Of course, we ran back at once. And I have this mental picture of a man suddenly appearing from the caretaker's house beside the Grammar School. He'd been shaving, for he was in his white vest – and army trousers, I seem to recall – and had a face full of lather. Just the same, he beat us to the spot. There was no explosion, and no fire, but I can still conjure up the smell of electrical burning from the wires where the wing had been torn off.'

Mr Maurice Hobson, and the caretaker's house

Mr Geoff Anderson, of Wath Upon Dearne, was rather closer to the action. Even so, having been approached, he paused. 'All these years', he said wonderingly, then, 'and nobody's ever asked me about it before! Yet when I've mentioned a Lysander putting down hereabouts people've looked at me gone out.'

Mr Geoff Anderson

He thought back. 'I was eleven, and being wartime we used to go home at dinner time. So we looked around to see this Lysander descending into the playing fields. He touched down well into the field, but then seemed to keep going, bouncing quite a bit, with his wings rocking. He didn't seem able to stop. Then he went through a thin wooden fence – and yes, there was a wall, of course, and a gap in it: I'd forgotten that! Then one wing caught this tree – the only tree around – and the plane slewed about and stopped. The pilot got out, I remember, and couldn't have been more than shaken, for we saw him making his own way over to the houses in Fitzwilliam Street where he was taken in at Frank Wade, the builder's, and looked after.' Mr Anderson reflected again. 'I never saw any guards, so I suppose, after a while, we just carried on home for dinner.'

Mrs Sheila Thompson, destined to become a teacher at the Grammar School, also a local artist, and still living in what had been Mr Frank Wade's house, also recalled the crash. 'I remember', she smiled, 'that both Cliff and Frank Wade ran out into what was then just a cornfield, thinking they'd be grappling with a German.'

The RAF court of inquiry was not impressed by Pilot Officer Chaldecott's handling of the incident. In detail, his commanding officer castigated him for 'carelessness, for failing to watch the weather, for not having obtained a met forecast, and for having failed to keep a navigational log'; but, above all, for not appreciating that he had chosen to land his valuable machine downslope on a snow-covered surface. The Air Officer Commanding No. 71 Group, however, no doubt knowing that the ex-soldier would have been feeling badly enough even before being 'torn off a strip' by his squadron commander (to say nothing of the ribbing his fellow pilots would have subjected their pet 'brown-job' to), decreed that the matter need be taken no further.

Mr Maurice Hobson indicates the tree which took off the wing, with Festival Road beyond

Mr Hobson brought the story up to date. 'In 1951 – Festival of Britain year – Festival Road was built along what had been just a footpath. Then, in about 2005 the Grammar School was demolished. But even by then the Wath Comprehensive School had been built across the space that was available for his landing run.'

The task of identifying the particular Pilot Officer Chaldecott concerned, and then tracing his future career, was eased by information independently furnished by air historian Mr Malcolm Barrass and author Mr David W. Earl from their *Air Force List* and *London Gazette* sources. From which it seems that, after the crash at Wath, Pilot Officer Algernon Chaldecott then applied himself to the task in a way that could only have pleased his commanding officer, for with this shaky downhill start behind him, things took what was to be a prolonged upturn.

Just two months after the crash, he was promoted to flying officer, being gazetted on 7 March 1941. Another promotion followed, but the second braid of his flight lieutenancy could hardly have lost its rawness before the two were eased apart by the thin ring lifting him to the senior-officer status of squadron leader. And barely a year later, on 7 March 1942, he was promoted yet again, to wing commander – if only to the temporary rank, and almost certainly without a regular wing commander's pay! No mean progression, just the same, for an erstwhile pongo! Yet even better was to come, for, surviving as he had proved he could on the playing fields of Wath, he flew on, and with equal success, survived the war itself.

VISITING THE SITE

The site lies off Festival Road, but apart from the tree, and the house where Pilot Officer Chaldecott ran for aid, development has obliterated all else.

22. Westland Wallace
Holgate Boys Grammar School, Shaw Lane, Barnsley

SE 33250 06007 143 m

Unit and Station: No. 504 Squadron, RAF Hucknall, Nottinghamshire, Bomber Command

Date: 21 November 1937

Crew: two, uninjured:

- Pilot Officer George Greaves
- One other, unidentified occupant

Westland Wallace

Having been operating over a coastal bombing range Pilot Officer Greaves became lost in snowy conditions with a suspect engine and made a precautionary landing on playing fields at Barnsley Grammar School. Despite its wheel brakes the aircraft almost overran into a wire fence bounding a quarry, but the other occupant (intriguingly described by the *Barnsley Chronicle* as 'the 16-year-old co-pilot') jumped out and pulled the machine around. The field being far too restricted for a take-off, the machine was dismantled for removal.

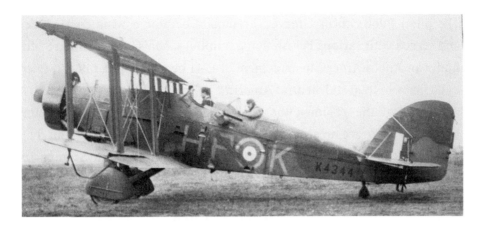

Jumped out and pulled the machine around

Mr Sam Heppenstall, of Barnsley, a former miner and police officer, recalled, 'It was a bright, sunny day and I was walking along Peel Street: I would have been 11 years old. The plane was obviously having problems as it was very low and had a spluttering engine. Then the engine stopped altogether. I followed on into Shaw Lane, and found that the plane had landed in the rugby field at the rear of the Holgate Boys' Grammar School. It was by the barbed-wire fence which surrounded a quarry. The rugby field is still there, but the school's a co-educational Sports College now.'

The Wallace's set-down area

The pilot, Pilot Officer Greaves, eventually became a wing commander and served with various British flying training schools in the United States under an Anglo-American agreement of 1941 by which RAF pilots trained as civilians in then still-neutral America.

Although the set-down was well publicised in the press, RAF Museum Hendon could trace no accident report summary for this aircraft. But that, though disappointing, is not altogether surprising, with so many summaries having been discarded as no longer of value.

VISITING THE SITE

When approached, the staff at the Grammar School allowed parking, and were helpful in pointing out the playing fields where the precautionary landing took place.

These are incidents which appear on enthusiast lists and websites, in books, and in popular lore, but which investigation has either shown to have no substance, or conversely, substance enough to keep on record for future research.

Miscellaneous

1. Junkers Ju88 of KG106

Service: Luftwaffe
Date: 3 July 1942

Ron Collier

This aircraft was recorded by *Dark Peak Aircraft Wrecks* author Mr Ron Collier, who might have expanded upon it had ill-health not intervened; he also named crew members Bergman and Majer, but gave no other details, and no location. It is entered here because, as Mr Collier was specific about the date, the unit, and the names of two crew members, it is possible that more information might be forthcoming in the future. Its inclusion also furnishes the present author with an opportunity to further acknowledge the debt owed to Mr Collier by all walkers who have puzzled over metal fragments chanced upon in their traverses of the Peaklands.

Dovestone Reservoir Area

2. Hawker Hurricane
Hoarstone Edge, above Dovestone Reservoir

SE 01316 01712 439 m

Hurricane at Hoarstone

In March 1978, when researcher Mr John Ownsworth undertook a search at this known Hurricane site, he found 'a bolt with a bearing, and some aluminium scraps'. Beyond that, nothing more is known of the background to this crash, which is recorded here for posterity.

3. Heinkel He111
Ashway Gap, above Dovestone Reservoir

SE 04000 04480 460 m (general area reference)
Service: Luftwaffe
Date: 16 April 1941

A German bomber is listed as having come down in this vicinity on 16 April 1941. No more certain location was available, however, and nothing was known of the aircraft by those approached in the area between 2004 and 2013. The general feeling is that this is a spurious report, although the specific dating lends some credibility. As with similar, rather nebulous reports, it is included here for a posterity in which archival or other evidence may be found.

VISITING THE SITE

It is hardly likely that any walker will visit this site for its own sake. However, if extending the moorland excursion north from the crash site of Lysander V9403 (Part One, Section 8, Page 71) or enjoying the far more worthwhile rim path above Greenfield Brook beyond Raven Stones, it might just prove of incidental interest.

4. Lockheed Hudson
Blindstones, south of Chew Reservoir

SE 03802 01286 536 m

Blindstones Moor

Enthusiast lists hold that a Hudson came down at Blindstones, and that wreckage existed for some time. Ranger Phillip Shaw, of Glossop, felt that fragments of aluminium found at the location given were from the water gauge detected many years before by veteran air crash-researchers Mr John Ownsworth and Mr Alan Jones. Just the same, in January 2007 permission was received for a party, shepherded by Peak Park Ranger Andy Valentine, to drive up the water-board's Chew Road and carry out a metal-detector search of the supposed site. Nothing was found, but at least the transport enabled Mr Ownsworth to take his poorly knee to the moors for the first time in twenty years. Not that his knee showed any appreciation of this kindly-meant outing over the next few days.

Ranger Dave Valentine and air-crash researchers Mr John Ownsworth, and Mr Alan Jones

5. Hawker Hurricane
Ravenstone Brow, Diggle

SE 02313 07800 248 m

Hurricane, Diggle

An enthusiast list has a Hurricane coming down at this location, but nothing else is known of the incident. In early 2012 no sign of debris was seen at the supposed site – on a steep hillside above Diggle Reservoir and just outside the warning markers of the rifle-firing range – and not even the longest-resident farming families had ever heard of an aircraft coming down thereabouts. The report, then, seems almost certainly spurious. What the upland approach from the Running Hill Head track does compensate with, however, is a panoramic view of the whole Tame Valley.

VISITING THE SITE.

Opportunity parking may be found a mile or so to the south-east of Diggle at the start of the Running Hill Head track at SE 01211 06796. Following this track north-eastwards for 800 yards then negotiating the disused Running Hill Pits gives a good view of the surrounding region, leading to Ravenstone Brow and the reputed crash site area after 0.92 of a mile (1.5 km).

6. Supermarine Spitfire
Irontongue Hill, Higher Swineshaw Reservoir

SE 01498 00599 408 m

Spitfire, Irontongue

Some sources hold that the debris of this aircraft was totally buried, but as far back as 1949 Mr Jim Chatterton, of Tintwistle, found 20mm cannon shells, as he noted, 'on Irontongue Hill, just below the summit, on the south-western side of the hill; a large, sparsely grassed area.' In the seventies, researcher Mr John Ownsworth spent a day metal-detecting the site with him but found nothing. Other searches up to early 2011 also proved negative, nor had any other details emerged from records. This is another site with provenance enough to be worth recording for a posterity in which more sophisticated detectors might advance research.

VISITING THE SITE

Routes to the area of this site are detailed in Part One, Section 4, covering Broken Ground (see above). This supposed site may not be enough to attract walkers onto this peaty moorland, but hopefully, the nearby Broken Ground site will, for the moorland vistas are both spacious and rewarding.

Woodhead Area

7. Unidentified 1914–18 aircraft
Air Shaft, Woodhead Tunnel

SE 14651 01850 415 m

Unidentified 1914-18 type, by the air shaft

1980's 'cuckoo' debris at the air shaft

Ranger Phillip Shaw, of Glossop, produced a transparency-derived photograph he took close to the tunnel in the 1980s showing a surprising amount of equally-surprisingly-complete debris – clearly an anorak jape. In fact, this was the period when researcher Mr John Ownsworth and his wife, Josie, trawled the area to no avail. Site visits up to early 2012 have been equally unproductive.

VISITING THE SITE

The Windle Edge Road (doubling here as the Trans Pennine Trail) to Dunford Bridge leaves the A628 Glossop-Sheffield Road at SE 14090 00547. Limited lay-by roadside parking can be found at SE 14871 01463 where a north-westerly track leads off towards one of the air shafts from the Woodhead Tunnel, the necessity to negotiate Smallden Clough making it a 500 yard walk. The reputed crash site is in this area. Although nothing is to be seen, bar the air shaft, that in itself might serve as a short-stroll picnic destination while the moorland area beyond it is well worth any walker's time.

Wessenden Head Moor

8. Avro Lancaster
Wessenden Head, east of Wessenden Head Reservoir

SE 16542 13643 164 m

This reputed site, just yards off the A635, appears on some enthusiast lists, but is almost undoubtedly spurious. Certainly nothing was found up to 2013, and no archive or anecdotal evidence has ever come to light.

VISITING THE SITE

In vetting the supposed Lancaster site, adequate roadside parking was found at the junction of the A635 and the Wessenden Head Road at SE 07768 07323. What makes the stop worthwhile is inspecting the terraces of the former Isle of Skye Inn, just opposite the junction, a hostelry so well known to older generations of walkers.

9. Supermarine Spitfire
Wessenden Head Moor, north-west of Black Hill

SE 07493 05492 536 m

Spitfire, Wessenden

In the 1980s researcher Mr John Ownsworth and some colleagues took this reputed crash site seriously enough to spend a day metal-detecting, but found no evidence. Certainly nothing aircraft-related was to be unearthed in 2013. Nor was any archive evidence discovered. As with similar sites having such provenance, this one is recorded for posterity.

VISITING THE SITE

One reasonable routing to this site is detailed in Part One, Section 15, Swordfish P4223 (see above).

Holmfirth Area

10. Handley Page Halifax (probably spurious)
Cartworth Moor, above Holmfirth

Reference to this crash is found in two enthusiast lists. Canvassing the farms on the plateau in September 2005 and again in mid 2010, however, turned up nobody, even among the oldest and longest-term residents, who knew anything of this reputed crash; nor was anything discovered, in the interim, in the archives. Had the report held the aircraft to be either a Lancaster or Spitfire – the Allied types so commonly attributed to any crashed machine – then one might well be dismissive about this site. The Halifax, however, is hardly a common type to settle on; accordingly this reference is recorded with an open mind.

Barnsley Area

11. De Havilland DH82A Tiger Moth
Black Lane, Tankersley, south of Barnsley

SK 35105 99501 141 m

Unit and Station: Flying Training Command

Date: 1939-45

Occupants: unknown

Tiger Moth landing site, Tankersley

In the 1980s, when researcher Mr John Ownsworth visited the area, locals remembered a Tiger Moth setting down in this field to the east of Black Lane, although whether or not it was damaged was unclear. Subsequent canvassing visits for this series, however, bore no fruit whatsoever. Nor was any specific Tiger Moth indicated during archival searches. Another site then, for posterity.

VISITING THE SITE

The setdown occurred in the field beyond the church to the east of Black Lane. Parking can be found in the immediate area.

12. German Bomber
Tanyard Beck, Hoylandswaine, west of Barnsley

SE 26068 05939 170 m
Service: Luftwaffe
Date: 1939-45

Tanyard Beck

In the 1980s several long-term Hoylandswaine residents told researcher Mr John Ownsworth of this incident. By 2010, however, no one could be found who knew anything of it. The impact site was held to be at the junction of the drystone wall and double-wire fence at the bank top to the east of the infant Tanyard Beck. Again, by 2010, the south-easterly field division leading to the junction from beyond the gully had been obliterated, only a stump of wall remaining at the bank top.

VISITING THE SITE

Having parked along the Gadding Moor Road as near as possible to SE 25609 06093, the site lies 550 yards off across the fields on a heading of 109°M and on the far slope of Tanyard Beck.

13. Gloster Meteor
Dodworth, Church Lane Colliery's spoil heap, Barnsley

SE 31477 06295 151 m (spoil heap)
Unit and Station: No. 211 Flying Training School, RAF Worksop,
No. 25 Group, Flying Training Command
Date: 1950s

Dodworth Meteor

With enthusiast lists giving such details as the unit, station, and group, this incident demanded attention, the content holding that a Worksop-based Meteor crashed into Church Lane Colliery's spoil heap in the early 1950s. By 2013 the vast expanse of the Dodworth spoil heap was pleasantly tree-covered, with woodland walks, and even pastures on the summit: well worth a look! However, enquiries among ex-miners who had lived in the area throughout the fifties brought universal disavowal that an aeroplane had ever crashed at the pit. Many, conversely, were aware of the 1937 Gladiator crash at Hermit House Farm, a property since made remote from the former Dodworth pit by extensive excavations, not least those made for the M1 Motorway. No verification having been found for any such Meteor crash, it is, therefore, included here merely to save other walkers time. What seems almost certain is that Dodworth has been confused with Treeton, a Sheffield location, where Meteor WB108 did indeed crash into a Colliery spoil heap in 1954 (See *Peakland Air Crashes: The Central Area,* p82, also Derbyshire's High Peak Air Crash Sties, Southern Region, Section 8, page 43)

PART FOUR: INTRODUCTION TO AIR-CRASH SITES ON THE BOWLAND FELLS AND THE SOUTH YORKSHIRE MOORS

The Forest of Bowland (Bowland Fell), and the South Yorkshire Moorland

One of my aims in writing of air-crash sites is to entice fellow walkers into some of the splendid upper moorlands they would not normally visit. I regard the crash sites, in other words, as tragic – but instructive – geocaches, giving a focus to what were originally off-path moorland forays. How the tracks carved by walkers seeking out such sites in the High Peak have developed over the last twenty or so years is evident. And, of course, the security afforded by GPS has aided deeper penetration into the moors. Underlying all, however, is the freedom to roam which even in the Derbyshire Moors was only gradually expanded once they lost their status as jealously-guarded preserves.

In finalising this book, in late 2013, my notice was drawn to two kindred areas to the north of the High Peak, those of Lancashire's Bowland Fell, and the South Yorkshire Moors. Where air crashes are concerned these moors also took their toll of hapless aircrews. In general terms, however, they have not been opened up so long to walkers, 'private' notices are not infrequent – 'This path leads onto private land, carry on to …' –, and although there are fine major footpaths along ridges, many of those leading into the moors remain, at best, challengingly vestigial.

Where the air-crash sites are concerned, I swiftly found myself ill at ease with current enthusiast coverage, especially those accounts which deliberately withhold the location of the sites. It is as though a new preserve has been established to replace landed privilege, with largesse only granted to initiates: as in 'a walker, who we had given location details to enable him to find the site' (sic). Presumably another self-styled 'Air Crash Investigator'.

No such pretensions were embraced by those who did the real pioneer work in the field: in the Peak, Ron Collier, John Ownsworth, Alan Jones, David W. Earl, and Rangers Phil Shaw, Peter Jackson, and 'Campy' Burrows, all of whom helped wheedle the lost-for-years locations from the moors using just maps and metal probes. Certainly, they did not crassly judge the debris they disinterred by either quality or quantity: '*the condition of many parts is poor …*'; and '*not much remains … though for a P-38 it is not bad …*'

Nor did they essay knowledge they did not have: '*could catch out even experienced pilots, as was the case …*' when the pilot concerned (though an instructor) was demonstrably inexperienced. Nor too, did they use terms they did not understand, misemploying 'disorientated' in aviation as a synonym for lost (see glossary). Then again, the pioneer enthusiasts did not err in believing that flying into, or being flown into, a hill in cloud, of itself bestowed gallantry on anyone, rightly reserving such terms for farmworkers who risked their lives in attempting to save trapped aircrews.

However, discounting such niggles – easily enough remedied –, throughout my few walks in these areas I was always aware of a sense of remoteness now lacking in the High Peak. For not only was I traversing unfamiliar high moorland, with no tracks between crash sites! but I was doing so without encountering other walkers. And always, magnificent ridge walks, wonderfully scenic valleys, with intriguingly interlocking re-entrants, distant vistas, not least of the sea, vast areas of trackless moor, and many a dreadfully boggy bit. So, what a fell-walker's wonderland!

As another facet; as a walker unfamiliar with an area bearing so many privacy signs, being unaware of their currency and not wishing to offend, and therefore wonderingly seeking out distant access points, my brief venture into the area, in late-2013-early-2014, showed – as might be expected – that a courteous approach to residents not only led to interest on both sides – as ever, where is archetypical straw-chewing farmer! – but invariably saved unnecessarily weary miles of tramping tarmac roads.

Just a half-dozen sites, then, to represent both areas. With, of course, guaranteed coordinates. And all the usual provisos for safe walking in changeable-weather, high moorlands …

1. North American P-51 Mustang, AP208
Holdron Moss, Forest of Bowland

SD 60814 50767

Unit and Squadron: RAF Clifton, York, No. 4 Squadron

Date: 29 November 1942

Occupants: pilot, killed

Holdron Moss, Professor Sean Moran, and Mick Winfield

Aircraft was flown into the moor during a photographic sortie.

2. Boulton Paul Defiant Mk.I N1651
Hawthornthwaite Fell, Forest of Bowland

SD 57497 51585

Unit and Squadron: RAF Squires Gate, Blackpool, No. 256 Squadron

Date: 18th August 1941

Occupants: pilot, killed

Hawthornthwaite Fell, Mick Winfield

Aircraft was flown into the fellside during a night cross-country.

3. Lockheed P-38 42-12905, Dunsop Fell, SD 67404 54250
Lockheed P-38 42-12928, Baxton Fell, SD 66804 56378

Unit and Squadron: RAF Goxhill, Lincs, 83rd Fighter Squadron, 78th Fighter Group, 8th USAAF
Date: 26th January 1943
Occupants: pilot in each, killed

P-38 42-12905, Dunsop Fell, Professor Sean Moran

P-38 42-12928 Baxton Fell, Mick Winfield at upper site

*P-38 42-12928 Baxton Fell, Sean Moran and lower site, Mick
Winfield, beyond, at upper site*

Aircraft collided and crashed after ferrying formation encountered cloud.

Despite the aforementioned, and derided, 'a walker, who we had given location details to', (sic) fine investigative work here by enthusiast groups *co-operating* to determine which aircraft was which.

4. Consolidated B-24J Liberator 42-100322
Burn Fell, near Slaidburn, Clitheroe

SD 67108 53167, impact site
SD 67200 53179, terminal site
Unit and Squadron: RAF Seething, 714th Bombardment Squadron, 448th Bombardment Group, 8th USAAF
Date: 2 January 1945
Occupants: nineteen, four killed, fifteen survived

Burn Fell, Sean Moran, impact site

Burn Fell, Self, terminal site

Aircraft, under full control and in stable flight (crew were uncertain of position in cloud, but not disorientated), was flown into the flat hilltop in cloud.

5. Bristol Blenheim Mk.5 BA246
Bleasedale Fell, Forest of Bowland

SD 57921 48244, panels

SD 57938 48244, undercarriage

Unit and Squadron: RAF Woodvale, Southport, No. 12 (Pilots) Advanced Flying Unit

Date: 9 August 1944

Occupants: instructor and pupil, both killed

Sean Moran, panel site

Self, undercarriage site

Aircraft was flown into the moor in poor weather during a dual night-flying exercise.

6. Consolidated B-24J Liberator 42-50668
Black Hameldon, Worsthorne Moor, above Todmorden

SD 91180 30046

Unit and Squadron: RAF North Pickenham, Norfolk,
854th Bombardment Squadron, 491st Bombardment Group, 8th USAAF.

Date: 19th February 1945

Occupants: eleven: five killed, three died of injuries, three injured.

B-24J Liberator, 42-50668, Black Hameldon

Aircraft, routing at too low an altitude, was flown into high ground.

'DARKY' EMERGENCY HOMING, AND ASSOCIATED EQUIPMENTS

Transmitter Receiver TR9, fighters

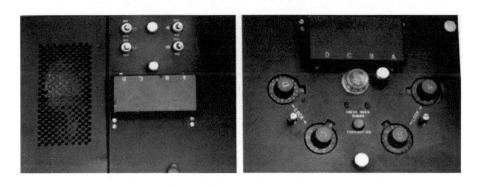

Transmitter Receiver 1196, multi-crew aircraft

Throughout this series various emergency 'get-you-home' systems are mentioned, and 'Darky' in particular. This was a quintessentially British facility which made a strength out of the limited, twenty-five mile range of the airborne R/T (voice) radio installations of the day, the Transmitter Receiver TR9s and TR1196s carried by fighters and multi-crew aircraft respectively. The facility was operated at RAF stations, but also at certain Royal Observation Corps posts, button 'D' being the emergency channel on which a lost aircraft could transmit blind for 'Darky'. Any listening post hearing the call would respond with its position, thus furnishing the aircrew with a location accurate to twenty-five miles, often enough to enable them to plot a course for base. Alternatively, especially if the aircraft needed to land quickly, the ground station could pass it the course to the nearest airfield. The ground station would then phone the adjoining listening post in that direction, who, when it heard the aircraft call, would take over and refine the lead-in.

Among non-radio aids were 'Occults', aerial lighthouses radiating a white, periodically-shaded (or occluded) light flashing a single identifying letter, and visible at 30 miles, which could direct their beams towards the nearest airfield.

'Granite' was supplementary to both facilities, the station sending off red flares to show its position, or alternatively to warn of high ground.

By the end of hostilities the Royal Observer Corps proudly claimed that over 7,000 Allied aircraft were saved by use of such systems, with 1,800 other damaged machines being guided to safe landings.

DO GHOSTLY AVIATORS HAUNT PEAKLAND'S MOORS?

It would seem that all desolate places stir up a certain disquiet in the human psyche. So perhaps the media's otherwise unaccountable readiness to dally with specious accounts of spectral aircraft crashing in the Peaklands is attributable to some deep-seated visceral unease. More simply discounted are the vaporous web utterances on Ghostly Planes, for these immediately disbar themselves by their so-evident lack of serious research.

Yet major search operations have indeed been mounted in the Peaklands for aircraft reported to have crashed, of which no trace was ever found; not only that, but the alerts have been initiated by concerned, level-headed persons. So, provided that each of these considerations is researched no further, it might well seem that, if phantasmal aviators do not wing the Peakland skies, then the wicked Big Brother Ministry of Defence must be engaged in some dark, high-moorland conspiracy.

Then again, one's natural bent towards the arcane might argue that, in the Peaklands, where so many aircraft have crashed with the loss of a substantial number of lives (albeit nowhere near as many as on the region's roads), it is only reasonable to expect some mystic forces to be operating. After all, everyone loves a ghost story, not least a sceptical fell-walker-aviator; although it is hazarded that most would find the *divertissement* a little less attractive on an upper moorland with the weather bleakly closing in and the light rather too rapidly fading.

One of the fundamentally unsound web articles interested itself in the Broomhead Moor operation of 27 March 1997, mounted after a widely reported moorland explosion. Here, the histrionic spin applied was to imply that the authorities had been mystified to find no wreckage. Yet there was no mystery to those involved. So that both Ranger Josef Hergi and his former mentor, Mr John Campion Barrows – 'Campy' – found the search perfectly logical, but the puerility of the superstitious lobby utterly unfathomable.

'The gamekeeper and his wife who reported the explosion,' Ranger Hergi reasoned, 'and all the others who phoned in, knew it hadn't been thunder, or a quarry detonation. We thought it had been a sonic boom, for we'd established that no aircraft were missing. Just the same we had to make certain it hadn't been a crash. But there was nothing inexplicable about it, still less a cover-up. And what could the Ministry of Defence do but reiterate that their pilots were forbidden to break the sound barrier over land? You could hardly expect the crew concerned to own up to it!' [Allowing that the crew in question had even been aware of directing a boom towards the ground: given the right in-flight parameters it only takes the tiniest forwards twitch of the stick!]

Certainly, the log of the Buxton Mountain Rescue Team ends its summary of the search call-out with the wryly derisive note, 'The media speculated that this was a "ghost aircraft" from WW2'.

But before getting overly bound up with wondering whether spectral aircraft just might exist, it has to be appreciated that sophisticated terrain-avoidance avionics enable aircraft to fly very fast and very low across the Peakland moors, by night and day, and in all weather conditions. Only even accepting such intellect-bedazzling technology, it seems to be an ineradicable trait of the Freudian id that it insists upon inventing spectres. As this former aviator discovered in the course of flying with several generations of otherwise well-balanced air hostesses who discovered ghosts in nearly every hotel room they were allocated. On occasion, to ease the minds of the poor misguided dears, he would change rooms with them. Of course, it took some time to sink home that in doing so he was exchanging a captain's executive suite, bowl of fruit, and luxurious bathroom – with fluffy towels and bidet – for a basic cell lacking all fripperies.

But what of the barren Peaklands? So many aircraft lost! So many young lives cruelly and untimely extinguished! Can anyone doubt that some unquiet spirits among them might indeed haunt the moors where they crashed?

Well, setting aside his naivety in exchanging rooms with less-than-truly-susceptible young women, this aviator-walker certainly can.

For the Peaklands have been peopled since the dawn of time; so that even the eponymous Pecsaeton ('*peek*-seeton': hence Peak!) tribe were relative latecomers. But mortality in the United Kingdom runs at some 629,500 a year, the rate in the Peakland moors area being 9.6 in every thousand of its population. From which it follows that if even a proportion of unquiet spirits decided to roam – especially once augmented by the district's erstwhile road users – there would be no vacant spaces on Kinder, and precious few on any other moor. What chance then, amid that ruck, for a paltry few-score of Johnny-come-lately airmen to find elbow room?

So where is the logic in this lurid sentimentalism that conjures up spectral aviators? For bearing in mind that the vast majority of crashes are caused by fallible human beings doing jobs as mundane as maintaining and driving a car, and simply getting it wrong, any lingering spirit-aviators would be far more inclined to hang their heads than to flaunt themselves.

When asked about spectres, Mr Peter Jackson had concurrently amassed thirty-six years as a part-time ranger and twenty-seven years as a mountain-rescue team volunteer; additionally, as a career police officer his beat had been the Snake and Derwent Valleys; also the Longdendale Valley – the 'haunted valley', as ghost-monger votaries would have it. In all that time he recalled only one near-ghostly experience. 'I'd taken a TV crew,' he explained, 'to a wartime crash site. Their presenter made her way into shot through the mist-wreathed wreckage declaiming, "I'm walking through a graveyard – an *aeroplane* graveyard – where for years now many people have reported seeing ghostly ..." Which I knew to be blatant fabrication.'

Ranger Jackson paused. Then said feelingly, 'I've walked these moors by day, and by night too, all my life, and I must have come across every phenomenon the imagination could conjure up. But never one that relied upon ghosts for an explanation.' He paused again, before expostulating with more than just a touch of acerbity, 'These people who have to sink to manufacturing sensation! The truth being that the Peakland moors encompass many a truly beautiful mystique; but not a single mystery.'

AIR-CRASH MYTHS

High among the gratifying outcomes of researching this series was the substance given to tenets encountered during various Air-Crash Investigation and Flight-Safety courses. Among these were that witnesses do indeed have a very independent perception of any event, and that some really will believe that an aircraft they saw flown blindly into a hill was actually on fire well before impact. Another was that if an aircraft has crashed in open fields it will invariably be held that the pilot was trying to avoid the village, the church, the hospital, or the school; even though, given even a modicum of control, any open space has to be infinitely preferable to any structure.

Of course, the latter borrows authority from such headlines as, 'Pilot's Bid to Avoid Houses at Caverswall', notwithstanding that the Venom in question was demonstrably beyond control. Even a student pilot who killed himself and destroyed his Vampire while 'beating-up' his home was afforded much indulgence, 'The young man's gallantry saved our home,' a neighbour told reporters. As for the fatuous heading which a local reporter thought apt for the Central book of this series, 'Tragic tales of pilots lured to their deaths by the Peak's beauty'! Some beauty, that, to be capable of luring by night and through thick cloud!

Of course, histrionic headlines sell newspapers, but when required, the leads are swiftly re-vamped, so that after the airliner crash at Kegworth, the 'Captain Hero' of Day One unapologetically gave place to, 'Was the wrong engine stopped?' of Day Two. Personal perceptions, conversely, tend to be more firmly entrenched, so that two level-headed witnesses of an abandoned Vampire which simply dived into the ground in fifties Wildboarclough remain unshaken in their belief that it had been 'a fireball in the sky'.

There were other beliefs not encountered in courses. Among them that any wartime aircraft which crashed had been 'one of theirs' – a German. Alongside which any large aircraft 'of ours' is held to have been a Lancaster; any little one, a Spitfire. Although one gentleman positively asserted, 'It was a German Spitfire – but all the crew were captured by the Home Guard.'

Then again it is widely held that German bombs which fell in the moors were jettisoned by raiders 'trying to escape', their crews, presumably, having unaccountably turned timorous. The reality being that for a 1941 German crew to get a bomb even that close to blacked-out Manchester and Sheffield accorded well with the accuracy of the 1945 Allied bombing fleets who still dropped over half their bombs in open country.

It also became clear that folk have the most benign regard for fliers, notwithstanding that virtually all crashes are caused by their crews. Always accepting that when, for example, a pilot stops the good engine instead of the bad one, the fault lies with him and not with those who failed to provide a foolproof 'this-is-the-bad-one' indicator. Certainly, the public tend to militantly oppose any official finding of 'pilot error', preferring to endow pilots, it would seem, with a near-papal degree of infallibility. Yet flying personnel, whether Service or Civilian, with every facet of their operation being rigorously tested every six months, are never under any such illusion.

It also became manifest that, prosaic as flying has become, its aura of romance-tinged-with-danger is still undimmed. Not that many of Peakland's crashed aircrews were ever aware that they were in any particular danger, most air-crash-survivors being doubly taken aback on discovering that, rather than five minutes from their cosy, low-lying Lincolnshire station, they were on a high and remote moorland forty miles distant.

Gratifyingly, amid these narratives are to be found several 'Good Shows' where captains decided to abandon, having found no safe way in which to penetrate cloud. There are even a very few incidents where the aircraft actually failed their crews, among these being a Skytrooper whose wingtip crumpled in the air. However, that the vast majority of Peakland's foredoomed crews remained providentially oblivious of what cloud and darkness hid from them is too often ignored in enthusiast accounts. For example, in direct contradiction of the facts established by the official investigators, a popularised account of the 1937 Heyford crash in Edale has the crew aware of their peril and firing off flares in a desperate attempt to locate themselves.

But then this series, written from the professional aviator's standpoint, was unashamedly conceived as a deliberate counter to such accounts, the corollary being that there are no histrionics, no 'forgotten heroes of the skies', and few to be singled out for individual praise.

Yet praise is given, and heroism is duly recognised, with ready regret being expressed where no official recognition was given to that heroism. As was so often the case when farmworkers risked everything in an endeavour to rescue crew members from burning aircraft, selflessly choosing to discount the imminence of explosion. Only for the most part nobody knew of this heroism, for when the authorities arrived such homespun heroes simply returned to their farming tasks. Indeed, when just such a former farmworker was searched out his family had no inkling of how Grand-dad had spent that fraught fifteen minutes on a time-hazed wartime day. But 'good' VCs have been won in far less time, and with a risk to life not one whit less extreme. Then again, notwithstanding that police, rangers, fire-service, mountain-rescue teams and civilian moor-searchers attend even the most remote of crashes, in the 300-plus incidents covered in this series only three rescue attempts drew the official notice of a King's Commendation, with unofficial recognition being equally sparse, and with rarely as much as a 'thank you' being said to assuage the trauma after the event.

This series then, contains no mysteries, and certainly no fanciful hints of dark cover-ups, still less of conspiracy theories; nor are heroics entertained. And yet, all aircrew being volunteers, courage underlies each incident. But it was always an unstated courage, besides which few would have exchanged their chosen role– with smart blue uniform, chest-swelling aircrew brevet, and the lure of coloured ribbons – for such other alternatives to the army as labouring on the farm or in the factory; or – dread the thought! – being drafted down the coal mines. Still less, being directed to the domestic kitchen.

Research, however, also revealed a perennial perception of flying as hazardous, but glamorous. Hazardous, despite the fact that, 'Beats working for a living, doesn't it?' is a stock conceit to be heard on any flight deck, whether Service or Civilian. Yet glamorous, assuredly, for although it is common knowledge that cabin staff spend their airborne hours in chores not best liked by either nurse or housewife, recruiters are invariably overwhelmed by applicants only too eager, it would seem, to mop up vomit. But then it could be that fliers, as opposed to aviation enthusiasts, tend more to the prosaic than to the romantic. Or perhaps the flier has learned from the outset to keep his head, at least, firmly on the ground. 'Isn't it wonderful,' enthused a pre-solo colleague, 'bursting through the clouds into dazzling sunlight like this?' Drawing the curt response from his instructor, 'I told you to level out at eighteen thousand feet.'

Just the same, nothing seems likely to dent a public perception of the romantic aviator which embraces even those who crash, evidently seeing them all as intrinsically different from the hapless skipper of a crumpled Peugeot. But any aviator writing on the subject would be doing a disservice to Aviation should his work lend credence to such a perception. Accordingly this series deliberately eschews both the sensational and the emotive, fixing its aims instead on directing the interested walker-reader to the site and describing what happened while at the same time critically examining why the incident occurred in the first place. Yet every criticism is made with fingers firmly crossed behind the back, and crossed not only for 'self' – as aircrew denote themselves in their flying log books –, but also for those countless others who, unlike the Peakland sons of Icarus featured in the series, did not – and hopefully, will not in the future – come to grief within the Peakland bounds.

AIRCRAFT TYPES

This section aims to provide the moorland walker-reader with a (very) potted guide to the once-proud aircraft now represented, at best, by pools of debris. As for performance figures, published sources dealing with wartime aircraft often perpetuate values enhanced for propaganda purposes. But then even those quoted in *Pilot's Notes* incorporate a healthy safety margin, while flying any one of a line-up of a given aircraft type will show all such data to be merely representative. Then again, to avoid wearisome repetition, British aircraft invariably employed Browning, Lewis, or Vickers 0.303 inch (7.7 mm) calibre machine guns.

Airspeed Oxford

The 1937 twin-engined, wooden-framed, plywood-skinned Airspeed Oxford remained in RAF Service until 1954. A dual-controlled, general purpose trainer, it had a basic crew of three but could accommodate other trainee-aircrew depending upon the role.

Two 375 horsepower Armstrong Siddeley Cheetah Ten radial engines, or alternatively, two 450 horsepower Pratt & Witney radial engines, gave it a cruising speed of some 163 mph (142 knots) and a ceiling of 19,000 feet; range was 700 miles. It could carry practice bombs and a few had a dorsal turret with a single machine gun.

Armstrong Whitworth Whitley

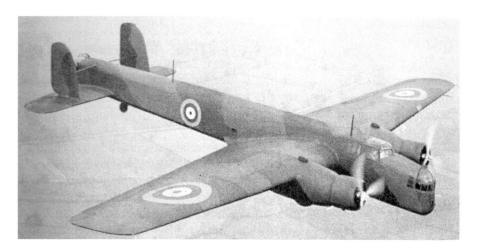

The 1936 five-crewed, twin-engined Whitley bomber was withdrawn from Bomber Command operations in April 1942 but served on in the training, maritime, paratrooping, clandestine-operations, and glider-tug roles. Most variants were powered by two 1,145 horsepower Rolls-Royce Merlin in-line engines. Performance is not that easy to establish as contemporary figures were subject to propaganda, estimates of the cruising speed varying from 210 mph (183 knots) down to 165 mph (143 knots) and as low as 120 mph! (104 knots). Even the service ceiling of 26,000 feet seems suspect. Typical armament was a single machine gun in the nose, and four in a tail turret. The bomb load was 7,000 pounds over a range of 1,500 miles.

Avro Anson

The 1935 Anson stayed with the RAF for twenty-two years. Conceived as a maritime reconnaissance aircraft, it was withdrawn from operational service in early 1942, after which it was employed extensively in the training role. As a dual-controlled machine with such innovations as hydraulically-operated flaps and undercarriage, it was used to train most aircrew specialisations. Normally accommodating between three and five, it could also be configured as an eight- to eleven-seat communications aircraft.

The Anson was well liked, being easy to fly, dependable, sturdy, and relatively forgiving. Its performance on one engine, however, was poor. It was typically powered by two 350 horsepower Armstrong Siddeley Cheetah Nine radial engines which gave it a cruising speed of 158 mph (138 knots) and a ceiling of 19,000 feet. Its range was nearly 800 miles.

Its design-role armament was two machine guns; a fixed, forward-firing Vickers, and a single Lewis in a dorsal turret. The nose had a bomb-aimer's station and 360 pounds of bombs could be carried.

Avro Lancaster

The seven-crewed Lancaster, developed from the twin-engined Manchester, first flew in January 1941. Designed for ease of production and subsequent servicing, 7,737 were built by 1946.

Powered by four 1,640 horsepower Rolls-Royce Merlin Mk.24 in-line engines, its maximum speed was 280 mph (243 knots), it cruised at 210 mph (182 knots) or, on three engines, at 140 mph (122 knots), operating up to 22,000 feet over a range of 2,500 miles. The standard bomb load was 14,000 pounds or, if modified, one of 22,000 pounds – for a comparison often made, the Flying Fortress's standard load was 6,000 pounds. The Lancaster's basic armament was eight machine guns; four in the tail, and two each in nose and dorsal turrets.

Avro Avian

The Avro Avian single-engined biplane, designed as a sporting, long-range racer, first flew in 1922. With two tandem seats in an open cockpit it was powered by a 100-horsepower de Havilland Gipsy I in-line engine, had an all up weight of 1,600 pounds, a top speed of 100 mph (87 knots), a cruising speed of 90 mph (78 knots), an initial climb rate of 600 feet a minute, a range of 360 miles, and a ceiling of 12,500 feet.

Boeing B-17 Flying Fortress

The Boeing B-17 first flew in July 1935, when its perceived role was that of a long-range outpost capable of defending America beyond the range of its shore defences, hence 'Flying Fortress'. However, after it was tested in action with the RAF such modifications as self-sealing fuel tanks and an increased amount of protective armour were called for. With these installed the B-17 then became the mainstay of the United States Eighth Army Air Force's bombing campaign which began in August 1942.

The enormous tail fin ensured that it provided a steady bombing platform at great heights, while the fact that it had formidable defensive armament, and that it proved capable of absorbing a considerable amount of battle damage, was held to make up for its relatively small bomb load.

The upgraded B-17G version relied for its defence on up to thirteen 0.5 inch, heavy-calibre machine guns, this fire-power being enhanced by the interdependent formation strategies employed. With so many guns to man, the standard crew complement was ten. This comprised pilot, co-pilot, navigator, bombardier, flight engineer, and radio operator. In combat the flight engineer would man the top turret, and the radio operator a swivel-gun in the roof of his compartment. The remaining four crew were dedicated gunners to man the ball-turret, the left and right waist positions, and the tail turret.

Typical performance figures for the B-17 reflect that it was powered by four 1,200 horsepower Wright Cyclone R-1820-65 9-cylinder air-cooled engines, with Hamilton three-bladed, constant-speed, fully-feathering propellers. This combination gave it a cruising speed of 225 mph (196 knots), a ceiling of over 40,000 feet, and a normal range of 3,000 miles. Its standard bomb load was 6,000 pounds, although this could be increased to 12,800 pounds, and over a very short range, to 20,800 pounds – for a comparison often made, the Lancaster's standard bomb load was 14,000 pounds, and it could be adapted to carry one bomb weighing 22,000 pounds.

Bristol Blenheim

In 1935 the prototype Blenheim proved faster than any fighter. By 1939, however, the three-crewed, twin-engined light bomber was outclassed by most German types but, although swiftly withdrawn from bombing operations, it served on as a radar-equipped night-fighter, and later as an advanced crew trainer. Employing two 905 horsepower Bristol Mercury Fifteen radial engines, the Blenheim Mk.4 had a ceiling of 27,000 feet, a cruising speed of 198 mph (172 knots), and a range of 1,460 miles. Armed with two machine guns in a power-operated dorsal turret, with two more, remotely-controlled, below the nose, and a fifth in the port wing, it could also carry 1,300 pounds of bombs.

Consolidated-Vultee 32 Liberator

Other designations: United States Army, **B-24 Liberator**; RAF, **Liberator**

The 1939 long-range B-24 Liberator was immediately ordered by Britain and France, with Britain inheriting the whole order when France fell. The type was first used by the British Overseas Airways Corporation and Coastal Command. However, by September 1943 the Americans themselves had come to appreciate its value. Over 18,000 were built, with the production rate reaching one every fifty-six minutes.

Four 1,200 horsepower Pratt & Whitney Twin Wasp engines driving Curtiss three-bladed, electrically-driven, constant-speed propellers gave a cruising speed of 220 mph (191 knots) and a ceiling of 36,000 feet. The range was 2,500 miles and the bomb load 8,000 pounds. Armament was up to fourteen machine guns of 0.5 inch (12.7 mm) calibre, in four turrets, and two waist positions.

De Havilland Chipmunk TMk.10

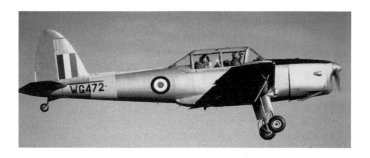

Designed as a replacement for the de Havilland Tiger Moth biplane trainer, the prototype Chipmunk monoplane first flew on 22 May 1946, paving the way for nearly nine hundred which were to be used by RAF training schools, by RAF Reserve units, and by University Air Squadrons. The single-engined Chipmunk had tandem seating for two – but to maintain its balance it had to be flown solo from the front seat – and a fixed, tailwheel-configuration undercarriage. Easy to fly in a casual fashion, it was an extremely demanding machine to fly accurately, while its spin occasionally showed lethal qualities. Just the same a delightful aircraft. And with a warm, enclosed cockpit, unlike the so-draughty Tiger Moth.

Powered by a Gipsy Major Mk.8 engine driving a two-bladed, fixed-pitch, metal propeller it had a maximum permitted speed of 199 mph (173 knots), a normal cruising speed of 104 mph (90 knots), and a stalling speed of 52 mph (45 knots).

De Havilland DH60M Moth

The first of the two-seater, single-Cirrus-engined de Havilland Moth biplane family made its initial flight in February 1925. The popularity of the Moth, not least with owners being able to fold back the wings for more compact stowage, was such that the Gipsy engine was developed, after which the type became generically known as the Gipsy Moth. The 'M' designation indicated a metal fuselage and was originally intended for the overseas market.

Representative of the type's performance was a maximum speed of 105 mph (91 knots) at sea level, a cruise of 85 mph (74 knot), a ceiling of 18,000 feet and a range of some 300 miles.

De Havilland Mosquito

The 1940 private-venture, twin-engined 'Wooden Wonder' Mosquito became an instant success with both the Service and the war-jaded public. Conceived as a fast, high-flying bomber which would need no performance-limiting defensive armament, the authorities had only tardily recognised its potential, the machine owing virtually everything to the faith of de Havillands.

The wooden construction was light, and saved on scarce alloys, while the 1,620 horsepower Rolls-Royce Merlin 25 in-line engines gave the Mosquito a cruising speed of 325 mph (283 knots) and could lift it to 33,000 feet over a range of 1,650 miles.

Not only was its performance outstanding, even when flying on one engine, but it proved itself the master of many roles: photo-reconnaissance, bomber, intruder, fighter-bomber, night-fighter, and communications-cum-freighter. Passing through many variants the type remained in RAF service until 1961. Crewed by a pilot and navigator seated side by side, the armed versions typically carried four 20 millimetre calibre cannon and four machine guns in the nose. It could carry 2,000 pounds of bombs.

De Havilland DH82A Tiger Moth

The 1934 improved Service version of the tandem two-seater biplane de Havilland Moth made an unassailable name for itself as a training machine at over 80 elementary flying training schools in the course of the Second World War.

Its 130 horsepower de Havilland Gipsy Major in-line engine gave it a cruising speed of 93 mph (80 knots), a ceiling of 13,000 feet and a range of 300 miles. For solo flight the pilot sat in the rear seat to maintain the centre of gravity, while a hood facilitated dual instrument-flying training. The machine could be fitted with bomb racks, and indeed, saw operational service both as a communications aircraft before the fall of France, and as a maritime scout.

Although demanding to fly accurately, it had virtually no vices; just the same, it brooked no undue liberties. Many still flew in 2013, and it is almost universally spoken of reverentially. It might be held as sacrilegious, therefore, to recall that its cockpit was uncomfortable, and that it invariably gave a freezing-cold ride.

Douglas DC-3 Dakota

The 1935 Douglas DC-3, the doyen of air transports, was still flying commercially in 2013. Carrying twenty-one passengers and a crew of three, it was variously known as the 'Mainliner', 'Silverliner', 'Flagship', 'Skyliner' and 'Skyclub', with its 'Douglas Sleeper Transport' version becoming the 'Sky-Sleeper' and 'Flagship Sleeper'. The RAF was to dub it the Dakota.

After the war many airlines gladly seized upon the DC-3. So that in August 1946, the restyled British European Airways finally painted up twenty-one DC-3 'Pionairs', having operated them in Service drab since their transfer from RAF Transport Command six months before. This version had an airstair door.

Typical performance figures for the DC-3 when powered by two 1,000-horsepower Wright Cyclone radial engines give a maximum speed of 220 mph (191 knots), a cruising speed of 194 mph (169 knots), a stalling speed of 67 mph (58 knots), a ceiling of 21,900 feet, and a range of 2,125 miles.

Fairey Barracuda

The 1940 Barracuda torpedo bomber with its retractable undercarriage and Fairey-Youngman flaps was a step up from the naval biplanes it replaced. When the Royal Navy took delivery, however, in 1943, the strengthening of certain components for deck landings and the addition of extra equipment meant that the Barracuda could no longer meet its design performance.

The 1,940-horsepower Rolls-Royce Merlin 32 in-line engine gave the production machine a cruising speed of 205 mph (178 knots), a ceiling of 21,600 feet and a range of 1,150 miles. A typical armament fit was two wing-mounted machine guns while the ordnance load was a single 1,620-pound torpedo or the same weight of bombs, mines, or depth charges.

Fairey Battle

Although relatively impressive when it first flew in early 1936, the single-engined Fairey Battle light-bomber was already obsolete by 1939 when war broke out. Accommodating a pilot, bomb-aimer/observer, and a wireless operator/air gunner, the Battle, powered by a 1,030 horsepower Rolls-Royce Merlin Mk.1 in-line engine, cruised at 210 mph (182 knots) at up to 25,000 feet and had a range of 1,000 miles. It could carry 1,000 pounds of bombs.

For defence it had a machine gun in a rear-cockpit mounting and another in the starboard wing. Just the same it was totally outclassed by the German first-line fighters, and after a series of gallantly fought, but disastrous, engagements during the German advance into France, the Battle was withdrawn as a day bomber. It continued to serve, however, in the training and target-towing roles.

Fairey Swordfish

By the outbreak of war the Fleet Air Arm's 1936 single-engined Swordfish torpedo-reconnaissance biplane bomber must already have seemed obsolescent. But with thirteen squadrons Swordfish-equipped it was inevitable that it was pressed into first-line service. And indeed it distinguished itself on several occasions, notably during the Norwegian campaign, and spectacularly when launched against the Italian fleet at Taranto in November 1940. Even as late as 1942 the venerable type was to show its teeth against major units of the German Battle Fleet, but the debacle that ensued forced its redeployment to the anti-submarine warfare role. Just the same, the Swordfish was not withdrawn from operations until May 1945.

Nominally a three-seater, yet for some roles reduced to a two-seater by the necessity of installing extra fuel tanks, the Swordfish, powered by its 750-horsepower Bristol Pegasus Thirty radial engine, had a cruising speed of 120 mph (105 knots), a ceiling of 10,700 feet, and a maximum range of some 1,000 miles. It was a surprisingly large machine, standing at over twelve feet when configured as a landplane, and even higher when floats were fitted.

Typical armament was a single Vickers firing through the propeller, and a Vickers or Lewis in the rear-cockpit mounting. Additionally one 1,600 pound torpedo or the same weight of mines, bombs, or depth charges could be carried.

Gloster Gamecock

As the 1925 Gamecock single-seater biplane fighter suffered from flutter problems, right-hand spins were prohibited. Even so it proved well suited to aerobatics. Powered by a 425-horsepower Bristol Jupiter engine it had a maximum speed of 155 mph (135 knots), could climb to 20,000 feet in 20 minutes, and had a service ceiling of 22,000 feet. It was armed with two fixed, forward-firing Vickers machine guns.

Gloster Gladiator

The 1934 single-seater, metal-framed, fabric-covered Gladiator, initially developed from the Gloster Gauntlet as a private venture by Gloster's designer, Mr Henry Folland, was to be the RAF's last biplane fighter.

Typically powered by an 840-horsepower Bristol Mercury Nine radial piston engine, it had a maximum speed of 255 mph (222 knots), cruised at 210 mph (182 knots) and could climb to 20,000 feet in 9.5 minutes. It had a ceiling of over 30,000 feet, a range of 440 miles, and an endurance of two hours. Armament was four Browning machine guns.

Gloster Meteor

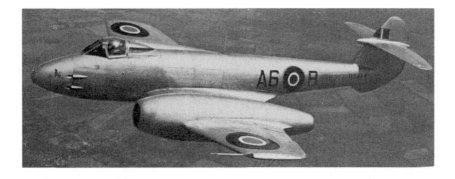

Though celebrated for being the only Allied jet aircraft to see service during the Second World War, developmental delays meant that the 1943 machine was not delivered until July 1944. After that, however, armed with four 20 mm calibre cannon, the twin-jet was successfully deployed against the V1 pulse-jet Flying Bombs.

Variants included a 1948 two-seater trainer and a 1949 two-crew night-fighter, with modifications including Martin Baker ejection seats.

Early versions were powered by two Rolls-Royce Welland turbojet engines, each developing 1,700 pounds of thrust to give a top speed of 415 mph (361 knots) and a ceiling of 40,000 feet. Later versions, fitted with Rolls-Royce Derwent Eight engines, each giving 3,660 pounds of thrust, brought the speed up to nearly 600 mph (521 Knots) and gave an initial rate of climb of 7,350 feet a minute.

Handley Page Halifax

The 1940 seven-crewed, twin-finned Halifax heavy bomber proved very versatile, being alternatively employed in both the transport and maritime roles, also as an ambulance, a glider tug, and as a clandestine and paratroop-delivery vehicle. An unfortunate characteristic of early marks was that fully-laden aircraft could enter an inverted, and effectively uncontrollable, spin. Modification of the tailfin leading-edge shape from triangular to quadrilateral helped overcome this stability defect.

A typical fit of four 1,615 horsepower Bristol Hercules Sixteen radial engines gave a cruising speed of 215 mph (187 knots) and a ceiling of 24,000 feet. It had a range of 1,030 miles, could carry 13,000 pounds of bombs, and mounted nine machine guns, one in the nose, and four each in dorsal and tail turrets.

Handley Page Hampden

The 1936 four-crewed Hampden, powered by two 1,000 horsepower, 9-cylinder, Bristol Pegasus Mark Eighteen radial engines, equipped ten RAF bomber squadrons at the outbreak of war. Here, though, is a case where propaganda-enhanced performance figures refuse to lie dormant. So, the Hampden's ceiling is frequently given as 19,000 feet, although Handley Page themselves only claimed 15,000 feet. At the same time, the company extolled their product's 'incredibly fast' 254 mph (221 knots) maximum speed. But although a 1942 source gives the cruise as 217 mph (189 knots), actual users found the workaday cruise to be nearer 130 mph (113 knots), with the least sanguine modern source proffering 167 mph (145 knots).

Irreconcilable figures aside, the Hampden's Handley Page leading-edge slots did give it a landing speed of just 73 mph (64 knots), and most sources agree that it had a range of 1,885 miles with half a bomb load, reducing to 1,200 miles when the full 4,000 pounds was carried. As defensive armament it had two forward-firing machine guns, with additional twin mountings in both a dorsal and a rearward-facing belly position.

The Hampden showed up poorly against German fighters, however, and just a month into the war it was restricted to night operations, to leaflet dropping, and to minelaying. Although the Hampden was regarded as pleasant to handle, the crew found their positions cramped.

Handley Page Heyford

The 1933 twin-engined, basically four-crewed Heyford was a biplane-bomber of all-metal framed construction whose speedy 143 mph (124 knots) earned it the appellation, 'Express'. Indeed, unlikely as it seems, a No. 102 Squadron Heyford was publicly looped during the 1935 Hendon Air Show! Interestingly too, it was held – admittedly by Handley Page – that, in comparison to a retractable undercarriage, the lighter weight of the streamlined but fixed undercarriage so minimised drag that it actually enhanced the Heyford's performance. Withdrawn from first-line service in 1939 the type still gave good value as a crew trainer until 1941, being stable, and pleasant to fly.

Powered by two 575 horsepower, Rolls-Royce Kestrel Mk.3 engines, the Heyford had a ceiling of 21,000 feet. Its full bomb load was 3,500 pounds and with half that load it had an operational striking range of 920 miles, or as Handley Page 'spin' preferred, it 'carried a very large load of bombs for 2,000 miles'. For defensive armament it carried three Lewis machine guns mounted respectively in dorsal, ventral, and nose positions.

Hawker Hurricane

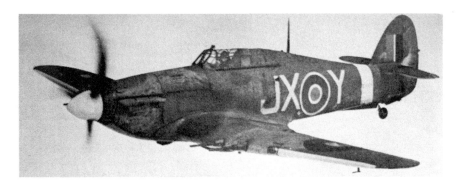

In 1933, when Hawkers conceived this now-celebrated monoplane fighter, the British authorities were still suspicious of all but biplanes, a prejudice dating back to the failure of one of *Monsieur* Blériot's monoplane designs back in 1912. The Blériot problem had been swiftly solved, but two subsequent British monoplane crashes, none of the three in the least connected, had led to the British Army – but not the Royal Navy – banning all its pilots from flying monoplanes. Indeed, it was Hawkers, rather than Authority, who ensured that by the outbreak of the Second World War the RAF had nineteen Hurricane squadrons – and just nine of Spitfires! Like the Spitfire, however, the Hurricane was to undergo constant modification until it was retired in 1947.

Typical performance details have the 1,280 horsepower Rolls-Royce Merlin Twenty in-line engine giving the Hurricane a maximum speed of 342 mph (297 knots), a cruise of 296 mph (257 knots), an initial climb rate of 2,700 feet a minute, and a ceiling of 36,500 feet. It had a range of 480 miles, or 985 miles with external fuel tanks, the fighter-bomber version carrying twelve forward-firing, wing-mounted machine guns and a 500 pound bomb load.

Heinkel He111

The 1935 Heinkel He111 ('One-eleven') was blooded with the Condor Legion in the Spanish Civil War, and later in Poland, handsomely outstripping the opposing fighters. Over Britain, however, both its armament and performance proved inadequate, particularly as German fighters were unable to dwell long enough to provide meaningful support. From mid-September 1940, therefore, it was restricted to night-time operations.

Powered by two 1100 Junkers Jumo engines it had an average speed (collating various sources) of 250 mph (217 knots), a ceiling of 23,000 feet, and a range of 1,030 miles. Early versions had a crew of four, a bomb load of some 4,000 pounds and three 7.9 mm calibre machine guns mounted dorsally, in the nose, and in a belly turret.

Junkers Ju88

Fortunately for the Allies, German aircraft designers, like their British counterparts, frequently had changes forced upon them. The 1939 Junkers Ju88 bomber, for example, was envisaged as a fast, minimally-armed machine capable of targeting the whole of the British Isles. In the event, the Luftwaffe's insistence that it be used primarily as a dive bomber called for a more robust construction. This increased the weight and reduced the design speed and manoeuvrability, reductions which called for more defensive armament. The bitter pill – to its crews – being that the type was never actually used as a dive-bomber except when operating over water!

The type was adapted to many roles but representative were two 1,400 horsepower Junkers 211J liquid-cooled inverted V12 engines which gave a maximum speed of 295 mph (256 knots) and a ceiling of 26,900 feet. Its four crew comprised pilot, bomb aimer, top-gunner/radio-operator, and lower-gunner/flight-engineer. The pilot controlled a 7.9 mm calibre machine gun with the gunners fighting three of 7.9 mm calibre and one of 13 mm calibre. Four 1,000 kilogram bombs could be carried.

Lockheed Hudson

The twin-engined, twin-finned, five-crewed Lockheed Hudson was the military version of the Lockheed 14 Super-Electra airliner, the RAF ordering 200 in June 1938. The order caused outrage among those who believed that buying any but British aeroplanes was heinous, a pernicious and far too long-lived lobby fortunately overruled on this occasion so that over 2,000 Hudsons were timely received, most flown over the Atlantic under their own power.

Intended as a navigational trainer, the Hudson was pressed into the maritime-reconnaissance and anti-submarine roles, carrying an air-droppable lifeboat while on air-sea rescue duties. It was also used as a bomber, and as a clandestine delivery vehicle for supplies and agents. Finally, once superseded as a first-line aircraft, it served as both trainer and transport.

Typically powered by two 1,100-horsepower Wright Cyclone engines, it cruised at 170 mph (148 knots), had an endurance of six hours, a range of 2,160 miles, and a ceiling of 22,000 feet. Carrying between 750 and 1,000 pounds of bombs, it mounted five machine guns; two below the nose, a moveable dorsal gun, and a pair in the rear turret. It could also carry two beam-mounted (waist) guns.

Lockheed P-38 Lightning

The 1939 twin-engined, twin-boomed Lockheed P-38 Lightning fighter had a basic range of 1,500 miles, extendable to 3,000 miles using auxiliary tanks. This meant that fleets of Lightnings made Atlantic delivery flights under their own steam. Their range was of great value to the American bomber crews who, by 1943, were suffering increasingly from a lack of fighter support. Then again, hard-pressed ground troops found that the Lightning was able to dwell in support for an hour longer than other fighters.

Powered by a 1,090 horsepower Allison V-1710 12-cylinder Prestone-cooled engine, driving a three-bladed Curtiss electric constant-speed, fully-feathering propeller, the type had a typical top speed of over 400 mph (348 knots), cruised at 300 mph (261 knots), had an initial rate of climb of 2,850 feet a minute, and a ceiling of 40,000 feet.

Typical armament was a 20 mm cannon and four 0.5 inch calibre machine guns in the nose with a bomb load of 2,000 pounds.

Miles Master Mk.3

In 1935 the private venture Miles Kestrel showed a top speed of nearly 300 mph – just 20 miles an hour slower than the Hurricane – and seemed the ideal machine for easing the transition from the Tiger Moth and Magister trainers to the first-line Hurricanes and Spitfires. However, following a pattern only too well established even by then, so many modifications were called for that in March 1939, when the emergent Miles Master trainer first flew, it was a full 100 miles an hour slower than the Hurricane. It did, however, retain handling characteristics similar to those of the new fighters.

After engine-fit problems, the Master Mark Three received the 825 horsepower Pratt & Whitney Wasp Junior radial, which gave the tandem-seated trainer a maximum speed of 232 mph (202 knots) and a cruising speed of 170 mph (148 knots) while retaining the 85 mph (74 knots) landing speed of earlier marks. It also had a ceiling of 25,000 feet and a range of 390 miles.

North American P-51 Mustang

Although the RAF took deliveries of the Mustang in 1942, the Americans themselves were slow to appreciate their home-constructed product. In consequence they lacked a long-range escort fighter when their European bomber offensive began later that year, losses soaring whenever their limited-range fighters had to turn for home. Only in December 1943, when the Rolls-Royce Merlin-engined Mustangs arrived in Europe, could the hard-pressed American bomber crews rely upon fighter support throughout an entire mission.

A typical version, the Mustang P-51B, was powered by a 1,520-horsepower Packard Rolls-Royce Merlin V-1650-3 liquid-cooled engine driving a three-bladed Curtiss electric constant-speed propeller. This combination gave it a maximum speed of over 400 mph (348 knots), a ceiling of 40,000 feet plus, and a range of over a thousand miles. As armament it mounted six or eight 0.5-inch calibre machine guns, or four 20 mm calibre cannon. It could also carry 1,000 pounds of bombs slung underwing.

North American Sabre (American, F-86)

In the early 1950s the British-designed replacements for the by-then outclassed Meteor and Vampire fighters were suffering many developmental problems, so the appearance early in the Korean War (1950–53) of the Soviet MiGs quite discomfited the Royal Air Force planners. Under a mutual defence agreement, therefore, America made over 431 Sabre jets, many developed and built in Canada.

These had an Allison J47-GE-13 engine developing 5,200 pounds of static thrust to give a maximum speed of 679 mph (590 knots) and an initial climb rate of 7,250 feet a minute. Most pilots found the Sabre a delight to fly and many expressed disappointment when it was replaced by the early marks of the Hawker Hunter. Just the same, by mid 1956 Hunters had completely replaced the RAF's Sabres, both in Germany and in the UK.

Supermarine Spitfire

The Spitfire first flew in 5 March 1936 and by October 1947, when production ceased, had metamorphosed through over a score of variant Marks. The early Spitfire was powered by a 1,030 horsepower Rolls-Royce Merlin Mark Two in-line engine, driving a wooden two-bladed, fixed-pitch propeller. This gave it a maximum level speed of 355 mph (308 knots) and a cruising speed of 265 mph (230 knots). It took 6.2 minutes to reach 15,000 feet and its ceiling was 34,000 feet. The undercarriage and flaps had to be manually operated and due to supply difficulties only four – rather than the planned eight – machine guns were installed. None of this would give a complete picture, however, unless the superb handling qualities of the machine were mentioned.

Vickers Armstrong Wellington

In designing the 1937 Wellington, the celebrated Barnes Wallis used repeated junctions of Meccano-like alloy members to form a cocoon of great strength. This 'geodetic' – parts of a circle – structure was then covered with doped fabric. The operational crew of four comprised pilot, navigator/bomb-aimer, wireless operator/air gunner, and rear gunner.

The German defences soon took the Wellington's measure, after which it was switched to night bombing. However, Wellingtons were also employed in the maritime role.

A typical power fit was two 1,500 horsepower Bristol Hercules Eleven radial engines which gave a ceiling of 19,000 feet and a maximum speed of 235 mph (204 knots). Representative cruising speeds vary with source, ranging from 232 mph (202 knots) to 166 mph (144 knots). A former Wellington pilot suggested 173 mph (150 knots) with a normal bombing altitude of 12,000 feet.

The bomb load was 4,500 pounds and the armament eight machine guns; four in the tail turret, two in the beam, and two in the nose.

The Wellington continued in service until 1953 using the T.10 version which, with the nose turret faired over, was dedicated to the pilot and navigator training roles.

Westland Lysander

The 1936 Lysander was a purpose-designed, two-seater, army co-operation machine delivered to the RAF in 1938. By the outbreak of war seven squadrons were Lysander equipped but although some saw action prior to the fall of France, the use of First World War techniques and the fact that the enemy had air superiority, meant that losses were inordinately high.

As a consequence the type was withdrawn from first-line service but continued to serve as a target tug, and in the air-defence-co-operation and air-sea rescue roles. The Lysander, however, excelled as a clandestine delivery machine for the Special Operations Executive (SOE) where its short-field performance was well suited to landing supplies and personnel in occupied Europe.

With its cockpit standing fourteen-and-a-half feet above the ground the Lysander was typically powered by an 870 horsepower Bristol Mercury Twenty or Thirty radial engine which gave it a maximum speed of 212 mph (184 knots) and a ceiling of 21,500 feet. It had a range of 600 miles.

Westland Wallace

The Wallace was a 1931 development of the 1927 Westland Wapiti biplane bomber which had served with distinction, notably in Iraq and Afghanistan, and was also widely used by the Auxiliary Air Force as a day bomber.

Metal-structured and fabric-covered, with a Townend Ring – an airflow-enhancing device –, a lengthened fuselage, wheelbrakes and undercarriage spats, and an enclosed canopy for pilot and gunner, the general-purpose Wallace was powered by a 680 horsepower Bristol Pegasus 4 engine. This gave it a cruising speed of 135 mph (117 knots), a maximum speed of 158 mph (137 knots), a range of 470 miles, a time to 10,000 feet of 6.2 minutes, and a service ceiling of 24,100 feet. It carried two machine guns, a fixed

Vickers forward, and a swivel-mounted Lewis aft. An especially modified Wallace was one of two Westland aircraft which overflew Mount Everest on 3 April 1933.

AAF: under the agreement by which American armed forces operated in Great Britain, they merely tenanted RAF stations. For their purposes such stations were designated as [United States] Army Air Force (AAF) bases, RAF Debden, for example, being known as AAF 356.

Abeam: lying at right angles to the line of march. All things being equal, if an established path is followed until a crash-site is directly off one's shoulder, then the least amount of rough walking is required to reach that site.

Aircrew: on 19 January 1939, airmen aircrew (observers and gunners) were effectively afforded the status of sergeants, although the situation was not regularised until early 1940 when heavy bombers appeared. World War Two aircrew categories comprised: pilot; navigator [observer, pre-1942]; wireless operator/air gunner; air gunner; flight engineer [post 1941]; bomb aimer [post 1942]; air signaller [post 1943]. There was also the observer radio (radar) of 1941, the navigator/wireless operator category, and similar combinations involving navigators.

Bombs: in general, these become armed only when a time-delay mechanism has operated.

Brown job: soldier, to the RAF and the Fish-heads (AKA Royal Navy). Just as the RAF are Blue jobs or Crabs.

Circuits and Rollers: a 'circuit' – circuits and landings – involves taking off into wind, turning downwind parallel to the runway, flying past the airfield, then turning back, touching down, and rolling to a stop. A 'roller' (circuits and bumps), on the other hand, requires the pilot to touch down, and while running along the runway, to reconfigure the aircraft for flight, put on full power, and take off again.

Civil Air Guard: a government scheme, initiated on 23 July 1938, to provide a reserve of civil pilots, men and women, by subsidising flying training.

Clough: a water-carved ravine leading from an upland peat moor. Most Peakland cloughs leave the rim in a steep river of boulders which look daunting but offer many routes through. Any too-steep pitches can be circumvented by backtracking a few yards.

Convex: used of a slope. From the rim the slope bellies outwards, so preventing a view of the ground immediately below.

Darky: an emergency get-you-home service that made a benefit of the very short range of wartime voice-radio sets. Merely hearing an aircraft call meant that it was quite close to the listening station. Telling the aircraft where the listening station was located, therefore, might well give the crew information enough to re-start their own navigation. Conversely, the aircraft could be directed towards the nearest airfield, each telephone-alerted listening station en route refining the direction to fly.

D-Day: 6 June 1944. The invasion of Europe in the Cherbourg-Peninsular area.

Degrees magnetic: measuring a track on the map will give the true direction. Adding five degrees will give the direction to set on the compass. So, a measured track of 070° is set on the compass ring as 075°. (Purists – and enthusiasts – will blanch, but the rest of us will be tramping heather for no more than half a mile or so.)

Disorientation (spatial): essentially, once the visual horizon is lost, it is only a matter of time before we lose the ability to determine which way is up. Pilots are schooled early on to rely upon the attitude instruments and to fight off all conflicting sensations. Until experienced, it is hard to imagine how compelling such sensations can be, but failure to discount them and trust that the instruments are telling the truth has proved a major cause of crashes.

Dorsal: mounted on the top – the back – of the aircraft; as with dorsal turret.

EFTS (Elementary Flying Training School): basic flying was taught, but the unit could also be used as a Grading School, where aspirant pilots were allowed fifteen hours' flying during which their suitability for further training would be assessed.

Empire, or Commonwealth, Air Training Scheme: set up in 1939 to take advantage of the favourable flying conditions in various Commonwealth countries: discontinued in late 1944.

Feather: to electrically or hydraulically turn the blades of a stopped propeller edge-on to the airflow to cut down the drag, as with an oar in rowing. The propeller of a failed engine left blade-on to the airflow, and therefore, said to be 'windmilling', creates an inordinate amount of drag.

Flutter: essentially, a vibration set up in a structure by (aerodynamic) forces which respond with that structure's natural resonance and increase rapidly to become destructive. Hence Boy Scouts break step for fear of destroying bridges …

Forced-landing/precautionary landing: a forced-landing is a set-down caused by a malfunction which gives the pilot no option but to alight. A precautionary landing is one where the pilot decides that it is politic to put down, so permitting the choice of a suitable site.

Gee (Ground Electronic Equipment): an airborne radar system devised for obtaining fixes and for homing in bad weather. To obtain a fix, radar-derived signals were plotted on a lattice chart. For a homing, the coordinates of an airfield were dialled into the Gee set, after which one of the lattice lines passing through that airfield could be followed, the overhead being indicated when the other, intersecting lattice line was reached. For use as a let-down aid in cloud, heights were calculated against ranges, so that, for instance, when about five minutes from the airfield a descent would be commenced at some 120 knots while losing 250 feet a minute until the ground was seen.

Geodetic: the structure developed by aircraft designer Sir Barnes Wallis and employed in the Wellington bomber. In essence, it comprised triangular grids made up of aluminium strips to form a mutually-supporting shell of great strength. More properly, the component parts formed 'geodetic' curves (parts of a circle) on the structure, each element taking the shortest line across the curved surface.

GPS: global positioning system. The satellite navigation system is essentially an American military facility which was opened to civilians in 1983 after an airliner was shot down on straying into a prohibited area. In 2000 accuracy for civilian usage was markedly improved. Like a map and compass, however, a GPS repays study, after which it can be of inestimable value on the moor.

Gremlins: manikins whose *raison d'être* was to harass aircrew by creating technical problems. They appeared in 1940, got into print in the *RAF Journal* in 1942, indoctrinated fighter pilot Roald Dahl a little later and subsequently Walt Disney. Known to be 'green, gamboge and gold; male, female and neuter; and both young and old', yet there were fliers who thought them fictitious.

Grough: a water-carved gully in an upland peat moor, often 20 feet deep. The peat is soot-black, and just as greasy. Egress, however, is always to be found within a few yards. Groughs, when going in the right direction, can afford easy passage.

Hag: the basically firm heather or bilberry stretches of ground left by **the** deep-cutting groughs.

IFF, Identification Friend or Foe: an airborne equipment which is set to a pre-designated code. When interrogated by an air-defence radar this automatically transmits a response showing the aircraft to be friendly. IFF was originally codenamed Parrot, the proword (procedural word) Squawk living on in referring to the code to be set. Additionally, an Emergency setting displayed a singular code.

Link Trainer: a flight simulator originally designed in 1929 by Ed Link, an American organ maker.

Ministry of Defence: created in 1971. Formerly, responsibilities in the matter of air-crash sites lay with the Air Ministry and the Ministry of Aircraft Production (later, Supply). The existence of the Protection of Military Remains Act 1986 is acknowledged – if very sceptically –, but although this forbids unauthorised tampering with crash-sites it says nothing of Authority's moral responsibility for the countryside.

Mission (terminology): throughout the era embracing the Second World War, offensive flights against the enemy were termed missions by the United States Army Air Force and operational sorties – or Ops –, by their RAF counterparts. The standard operational tour required from RAF crews may be taken as thirty.

Oboe: a blind bombing aid employing two ground stations. Essentially, one provided a beam to lead the aircraft over the target, the other told it the bomb-release point. Using stations at Dover and Cromer, it was first employed against a Ruhr target on 21 December 1942 with an accuracy of some eighty yards. After the invasion twenty-four mobile stations were placed on the continent.

Q-Code: a three-letter brevity code employed for frequently-used messages when most airborne communication was by the ploddingly-protracted morse code. Some, like QGH (below), linger on in R/T usage.

QGH, or **Homing and Controlled-Descent through Cloud**: an airfield recovery procedure in which a ground controller using direction-finding equipment tells the pilot what to do, the pilot simply following instructions. The aircraft is homed to overhead the airfield, then turned onto a safe heading and given descent clearance. Once it has lost roughly half its height, it is turned inbound again, continuing its descent until it breaks cloud and the pilot declares that he can see the airfield.

Pilotage: navigating by map reading. The nautical usage, of a pilot navigating a ship to its berth, gives the sense. Although seemingly dated, the word was to be employed by the crew of the Apollo 8 moonshot in 1968, who recorded having had, 'difficulty in "pilotage", that is, in trying to plot our path on the map of the back side of the moon'.

Screening: after thirty ops crews were stood down from operational flying, although they might be recalled for a second tour. Screening was also used in the sense of monitoring a pupil.

Special Operations Executive (SOE): a organisation of volunteers set up in July 1940 to carry out sabotage and subversion behind enemy lines. Churchill described its purpose as being to 'set Europe ablaze'.

Standard Beam Approach (SBA): in essence, this was a radar landing aid which transmitted a 30 mile long, very narrow radio beam down the extended centre-line of the runway. This told a pilot receiving the aural 'on-the-beam' signal that he was somewhere along the projected centre-line of the runway. To furnish an exact location *along* the beam, an 'Outer Marker' radio beacon was sited at a known distance from touchdown. This sent a coded signal vertically upwards to tell an inbound pilot that he should commence his final approach, descending at a rate of 600 feet a minute.

Stick (control column): certainly, from the fifties this was always the preferred term among pilots; 'pole' was equally acceptable but somewhat informal, 'joystick' almost antediluvially archaic, and 'control column' too pedantic even for Central Flying School. So stick it is, even where the aircraft in question had a wheel, or a yoke.

Very pistol, sometimes **Very's pistol**: a breach-loading, wide-bored signalling handgun firing cartridge flares of various colours, named for its 1877 inventor, American naval officer Edward Wilson Very.

Wreck: a misnomer employed by air-crash enthusiasts seeking an elegant variation on 'air crash'. Any class of air-craft may be wrecked if it is on the ground but the nautical model, though legitimately transferred in the railway context, is misemployed for machines in flight. Wreckage, as a synonym for debris, fragments, and remains, is, of course, legitimate usage.

Yards/Metres: again, let purists go pale, but to the workaday walker these are interchangeable below half a mile.

ACKNOWLEDGEMENTS

To the pioneering, joint authors of the two *Dark Peak Aircraft Wreck* books (1979 and 1982) who paved the way for all walkers puzzled by metal fragments chanced upon while traversing the Peakland Moors. To Ron Collier 1935–2010: Ranger Phil Shaw, a field companion, remembers how Ron tramped the moors in the seventies 'with nothing but a compass, hearsay, and myths to go on, so that locating a site often took him weeks'; additionally Ron devoted twenty-five years to the Air Training Corps and qualified as a private pilot. To Roni Wilkinson, who, as an author of boys' stories, set the tone for Ron's findings, serialising the material in the *Barnsley Chronicle* and subsequently joining Pen & Sword Books Ltd.

To veteran air-crash researchers John Ownsworth and Alan Jones (a noted aviation artist), both of whom furnished much extra-archival detail. This also applies to author David W. Earl.

To Malcolm Barrass, whose superlative website *Air of Authority* (www. rafweb.org) is a never-failing and utterly dependable source.

To Paul Dalling, for editing the manuscript, and to Simon Hartshorne for creating the book.

To Clive Teale, aviator and grammarian, for technical advice. Similarly to Ken Johnson and Ken Clare for down-to-earth criticism.

To Professor Sean Moran, of Wirksworth, who supplied 'links' enabling the quality of enthusiast web-forum observations to be assessed.

To the several hundred folk interviewed, particularly from busy farming families, who gave their time to the research for this series.

To the RAF Museum, the Imperial War Museum, and to the British Library, for assistance with transcribing wartime map references to modern coordinates.

To Derwent Living, December 2010 (the coldest in 100 years): for no central heating, and memorable proof-reading in fingerless gloves. And to Derby City Council's Housing Enforcement Agency, who relieved my plight.

To the ever-ebullient – and consistently irreverent – personnel of the Four Seasons Café, Park Farm, Derby; The Wheatcroft's Wharf Café, Cromford; Caudwell's Mill Café, Rowsley; ASDA/Macdonald's, Spondon; Croots Farm Shop, Duffield; and in particular, Hobb's Tea Rooms, Monsal Head.

To the National Trust staff at Kedleston Hall for both irreverence and forbearance.

To the immeasurable expedition afforded by Google.

To the oncologists of Derby Royal and Nottingham City Hospitals who, early in 2014, advised me against waiting for mainstream publishers to put this book on their list, and not to start another long one, whether as author, or reader

To the traced copyright holders authorising the use of their photographs: Richard Haigh, manager, intellectual properties, Rolls Royce; Nicola Hunt, intellectual property rights copyright unit, MOD; archives staff, Imperial War Museum; Judy Nokes, licensing adviser, HMSO (Crown Copyright/ MOD); John Ownsworth, for photographs used by Ron Collier; Archives staff, Royal Air Force Museum; Mike Stowe, American crash reports; Julian Temple, archivist, Vickers' Brooklands Museum, Weybridge; and Toni Wilkinson, Pen & Sword Publishing. Craving the indulgence of those for whom all contact attempts have failed.

Despite such inestimable assistance, any errors remaining, and all opinions expressed, are my own.

Pat Cunningham, DFM

SELECTIVE REFERENCES

Air Ministry (1937) *Royal Air Force Pocket Book, AP1081.* London: HMSO

Air Ministry (1941) *Air Navigation Volume 1, AP1234.* London: HMSO

Air Ministry (1943) *Elementary Flying Training, AP1979A.* London: HMSO

Air Ministry (1948) *The Rise and Fall of the German Air Force (1931 to 1945).* London: HMSO

Air Ministry (1954) *Flying, Volumes 1 and 2, AP129.* (Sixth edition). London: HMSO

Air Ministry (1960) *Flying Instructor's Handbook,* AP3225D. London: HMSO

Barrass, Malcolm (2005) *Air of Authority* (www.rafweb.org), (RAF organisation)

Bennett, D.C.T. (1936) *The Complete Air Navigator.* London: Pitman

Collier, Ron; Wilkinson, Roni. (1979, 1982) *Dark Peak Aircraft Wrecks 1 & 2.* Barnsley: Pen & Sword

Cunningham, Pat (Peakland Air Crashes Series: *The South* (2005); *The Central Area* (2006); *The North* (2006). Ashbourne: Landmark Publishing

Earl, David W. (1995, 1999) Hell on High Ground series. Airlife: Shrewsbury

Fellowes, P.F.M. (1942) *Britain's Wonderful Air Force.* London: Odhams

Hammerton, J. (1943) *ABC of the RAF.* London: Amalgamated Press

Handley Page Ltd (1949) *Forty Years On.* London: Handley Page

HMSO (1942–1943) *Aircraft Recognition.* London: Sampson Clark

Hurst, Ian; Bennett, Roger, (2007) *Mountain Rescue.* Stroud: Tempus Books

Lamplugh, A.G. (1931) *Accidents in Civil Aviation.* Royal Aeronautical Paper, Institution of Aeronautical Engineers, 29 October 1931, London

Macadam, John (*c.*1942) *The Reluctant Erk.* London: Jarrolds Publishers Ltd

Monday, David (1982) *British Aircraft of World War II.* Chancellor Press: London

Office of Public Sector Information (OPSI) (2008) *Protection of Military Remains Act 1986, order 2008.* London

Phelps, Anthony. (1944) *I couldn't care less.* (Air Transport Auxiliary) Leicester: Harborough

Saville-Sneath, R.A. (1945) *Aircraft of the United States, Volume One.* London: Penguin

Stewart, Oliver. (1941) *The Royal Air Force in Pictures.* London: Country Life

Sturtivant, Ray; Page, Gordon. (1999) *'Air Britain Listings' series.* Old Woking: Unwin

Thetford, Owen (1958) *Aircraft of the Royal Air Force 1918-58.* London: Putnam

ND - #0193 - 270225 - C0 - 234/156/13 - PB - 9781780913735 - Gloss Lamination